COUNTRY LIVING

Country Color Combinations

COUNTRY LIVING

Country Color Combinations

decorating solutions for every room

KATE BUTCHER

HEARST BOOKS

A DIVISION OF STERLING PUBLISHING CO., INC.

NEW YORK

Library of Congress Cataloging-in-Publication Data Available

ISBN 1-58816-263-X

Published by Hearst Books
A Division of Sterling Publishing Company, Inc.
387 Park Avenue South, New York, NY 10016

Country Living and Hearst Books are trademarks owned by
Hearst Magazines Property, Inc., in USA, and Hearst Communications, Inc., in Canada.

www.countryliving.com

Distributed in Canada by Sterling Publishing
C/o Canadian Manda Group, One Atlantic Avenue, Suite 105
Toronto, Ontario, Canada M6K 3E7

Project Editor: Gillian Haslam
Copy Editor: Alison Wormleighton
Designer: Christine Wood

Reproduction by Classic Scan Pte Ltd, Singapore
Printed and bound by Imago, Singapore
This book was typeset using ITC Berkeley and Neue Helvetica

contents

foreword

by Nancy Mernit Soriano,

Editor-in-Chief, Country Living Magazine

Welcome to *Country Living* Magazine's *Country Color Combinations*, an expressive palette of decorating schemes inspired by the natural shades of landscapes and gardens. Throughout the year *Country Living* features hundreds of houses furnished in imaginative ways and distinctive colors. This book reflects many of those color schemes —from the rich greens and golds of woodlands to the cool grays and blues of the coastline; from the pastel blooms that fill country borders to the crisp hues of garden-grown fruits and vegetables. There's also plenty of inspiration to be found in the mellow neutrals of chalk, slate, stone, and terra cotta.

Color is one of the most expressive tools in decorating. We hope this look at *Country Color Combinations* provides you with both inspiration and practical applications. For more decorating advice, turn to the pages of *Country Living* every month.

Glowing walls and paintwork, random-patterned cushions, and the natural tones of wood and stone combine in a 17th-century farmhouse to capture the glorious variety of country colors. The contrasts are rich and dramatic, the textures subtle, and the whole setting offer a sense of comfort.

introduction

Country decorating is full of classic color combinations, some of them inspired by natural features such as flowers and foliage, others acquiring familiarity through traditional use — elegant blue and white china, crisp red and white gingham, and the mellow green and cream shades of old-fashioned kitchen pantries. The best combinations are effortlessly comfortable to live with, because they are inspired by natural sources where they already exist in perfect harmony. This book demonstrates why they work so well, shows you how to use them, and how to adapt them with subtle variations of your own.

Divided into five distinctive themes, it shows country rooms furnished and decorated in irresistible shades, along with sources of inspiration and practical information on how the colors influence each other, to help you recreate the effect for yourself. *Field & Woodland* captures the foliage, berries, and meadow grasses of the changing seasons. *Sun, Sea & Sky* plays with the contrasting character of cool waters and summer warmth. *Flowers & Blossom* provides a rainbow of hues from country gardens and cottage borders. *Kitchen Garden* mixes fresh, crisp fruit and vegetable shades with the domestic traditions of a farmhouse kitchen. And *Slate & Stone* explores the subtleties and textures of natural materials that we sometimes take for granted but which are, in fact, a treasure trove of elegant, restful furnishing colors.

As well as awakening your vision to the color possibilities, textures, and moods presented by different aspects of the countryside, each chapter offers a palette of ten shades from which you can create your own decorating plans. These form the basis for the rooms that follow, with further tints and tones being incorporated in each one to bring individual rooms to life, and contrasting accents showing how you can adapt them to suit different settings. The rooms themselves are full of natural inspiration, with selected combinations capturing specific country elements. Use them as your starting point to give your furnishing plans an outline structure, then experiment for yourself by drawing in colors from other themes and chapters. You'll find sympathies and similarities emerging — between the pretty pastels of the *Flowers & Blossom* and *Sun, Sea & Sky* chapters, or the moody grays of *Sun, Sea & Sky* and *Slate & Stone*, or the fresh greens of *Field & Woodland* and *Kitchen Garden*. Let these natural associations guide you from one palette to another, and you'll gradually acquire the confidence to mix and match between them.

FIELD & WOODLAND

FIELD & WOODLAND

GREENS, BROWNS, GOLDS, AND TERRA-COTTAS are traditional earth colors that appear naturally together in the countryside and are easy to live with in our homes. Their close affiliation is increased by the way the colors overlap throughout the seasons, appearing almost to contain one another as they shift from one shade to the next. Comfortable and relaxing, they work particularly well in living rooms, dining rooms, and studies, where their warm tones create a familiar and inviting environment. Look for inspiration among the pale greeny golds of ripening cornfields and the bright golds of hay bales. Add splashes of berry red to the polished surfaces of dark brown or green leather furniture.

Right: Bright, glowing crab apples and crimson rosehips provide a sudden flash of brillliant color against the natural greens of mixed woodland foliage.

Let rough, unfinished beams and floorboards recreate the mellow stripes of newly plowed fields. Use soft, muted mushroom shades to provide gentle highlights and restful, neutral backgrounds, or in combination with warmer shades to cool them down. Experiment, too, with deep, dramatic purply blues — an unexpected shot of cool amid all this warmth, but perfectly reminiscent of brambles and sloes. Enjoy the overwhelmingly natural effect that all these colors create as they intermingle, and reflect it by incorporating simple materials such as hand-thrown terra-cotta and earthenware, and including rough-woven linen and burlap among rich, comfortable velvets.

THE FIELD & WOODLAND PALETTE

These ten shades provide a basic palette for recreating the natural colors of the countryside. Use the stronger golds and russets for warm, autumnal settings, then add cooler, fresher accents with a range of greens, and occasional flashes of drama with bright reds and deep brambly blue-black. Pale yellows are restful as background colors, and neutral tones can be conjured up by the contrasting shades of soft mushroom or rich chestnut, depending on the effect you want. Let this palette inspire your initial color scheme, then draw in other variations from the combinations shown on the following pages.

mushroom

The perfect balance to all the golds, greens, and russets of the hedgerow. This soft taupe, cool but slightly pink-tinged, adds gentle contrasts against the richer shades and also supplies its own very usable color — the outdoor equivalent of coffee and cream. Try it in neutral, toned-down designs, and look for fabrics such as linen and burlap that provide this versatile color naturally.

wheat

The pale green-tinged yellow of the traditional cornfield. A muted gold with dark undertones, it can look subtly drab in quietly lit rooms or merry and yellow in bright sunshine. This gentle, restful color adds warm highlights to the rest of the palette and provides a mellow background for deeper tones.

hay

A brighter gold, full of sunshine and sparkle, that hovers between yellow and orange. Perfect for picking up the reflective highlights of gold paintwork and gilded picture frames, and also for creating a fresh contrast with bright greens and rich chestnut browns. A much hotter shade than wheat, it needs more careful handling, but is always warm and inviting.

lichen

A subtle and delicate silvery green that is incredibly useful — both as a cool, refreshing background shade, and to add soft highlights and details. Use it on woodwork as an alternative to white or cream, or to transform furniture with a coat of pale, Scandinavian-style color. Make the most of its almost neutral quality in elegant combinations with taupes, grays, and creams.

meadow

The fresh, bright green of spring and summer — far more energetic than pale lichen. An energizing color to wake up to, it's good for bedrooms as well as being a refreshing shade for kitchens and bathrooms. Because of its leafy associations, it also makes a crisp, pretty mix with the blues, pinks, and mauves from the Flowers & Blossom palette (page 76).

holly

A rich, glossy green with a distinctive sense of drama — perfect for formal dining rooms and book-lined studies. It is traditionally associated with winter, yet its evergreen character gives it a more durable quality than the rest of the palette: where the other colors shift and change according to the seasons, this green stays deep and atmospheric throughout the year.

russet

Pure fall in a single shade. This is a classic country color, reflecting the warmth of the traditional farmhouse kitchen, the changing shades of the seasons, and the natural character of materials such as wood, basketware, and terra-cotta tiles. It mixes beautifully with reds and golds, and offsets fresher greens to perfection.

berry

A glowing, jewel-bright splash of pure color amid the golden browns and yellow-greens of the hedgerow. Berry adds crisp, refreshing drama to the more muted greens, and also holds its own against the flame-tinged russets of fall. Use it sparingly for accents and details until you feel confident with it, then try it for sumptuous, inviting dining rooms and living rooms.

chestnut

The color of horse chestnuts, polished wood, and old leather, a rich dark brown that instantly sets a classic tone. Redolent of studies, libraries, and gentlemen's clubs, it has a drama of its own, but is also very comfortable. Use it to add deep, dramatic accents to lighter neutrals and bright reds and greens, and look for luxurious textures such as velvet and velour that match its rich tone.

blackberry

A blue-black purple that introduces a slightly different color tone to the Field & Woodland palette. Dramatic but cool, it is remarkably versatile, providing effective contrasts to the brighter reds, greens, and golds and also adding variety of texture, from the soft velvety blue of sloe and blueberry to the glossy black of wild brambles.

Far left top: A collection of patchwork quilts incorporates the bright reds, greens, golds, russets, and blue-blacks of the Field & Woodland palette and echoes the random mix in which they naturally appear. The painted cupboard reinforces the colors.

Far left bottom: Berry-red woodwork and bright-painted entry hall glow brilliantly against the rich, dark chestnut of a paneled wall and a polished leather sofa. A russet and gold rug and the more muted shades of the faded linen pillow provide natural balance.

Left: Soft terra-cotta walls echo the warm tones of freshly turned earth. It's a gentle, powdery shade with plenty of texture, which suits rough-plastered surfaces and provides a restful background for the honey-colored furniture and woven twig wreaths.

Above: Bright leaf green creates a dramatic background for pictures and statuary, reflecting the light to provide an atmospheric setting and a striking contrast with the reds and oranges of the kilim-covered chairs.

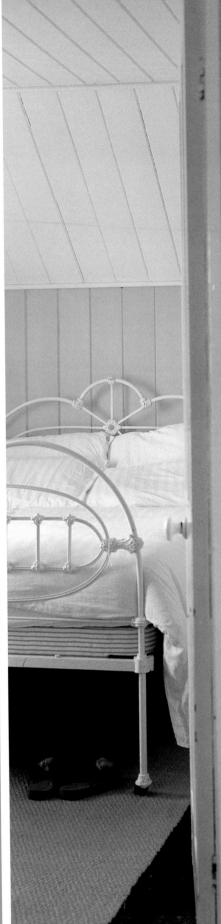

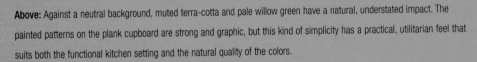

Above: Against a neutral background, muted terra-cotta and pale willow green have a natural, understated impact. The painted patterns on the plank cupboard are strong and graphic, but this kind of simplicity has a practical, utilitarian feel that suits both the functional kitchen setting and the natural quality of the colors.

Right: For a softer interpretation of fall colors, offset the bright gold and faded russet of turning leaves with pale silvery green shades of lichen. The painted paneling of doors and walls carries these colors beautifully, and coir matting adds natural texture.

Far right: Plain wood and natural basketware add their own color and grain to a woodland color scheme, toning down bright red and gold paints with a gentler, mellower touch.

Left: Contrasting greens conjure up the softness of early spring leaves, mixing pale and silvery shades with fresh yellow-greens.

Right: Ocher walls create a wonderful background for the natural earth colors of gold and brown, as well as deeper flashes of russet and blueberry.

Far right: Billowing curtains in ripe gold, hand-painted with flowing lilies, frame this small-paned cottage window.

Below: Chunky earthenware, in shades from dark glazed brown to pale matte clay, mixes comfortably on a kitchen shelf.

Below right: The pale greeny gold of foliage creates a gentle contrast with clay pots and pinky-purple flowerheads.

Below far right: This colorwashed wall layers russet over yellow, while the shade is striped in the colors of fall leaves.

hay & russet

Of all the glowing shades in the harvest palette, nothing captures the changing seasons of the country calendar like this glorious evocation of golden hayfields and autumn leaves. Suggesting the warmth of the late summer sun as well as the turning colors of the trees and hedgerows, it has a natural harmony that invites you in and makes you instantly comfortable. Here, pillows, covers, wood tones, and paint shades all work together as easily as the foliage of an autumn forest. Contrasting textures will help to enrich the mix, so combine polished wood furniture with simpler, waxed finishes; deep velvets with thick, textured linens and soft wool fabrics; smooth, flat eggshell woodwork with the layered paintwork of colorwashed walls. To bring out the simpler elements of the harvest theme, add unglazed earthenware, painted wood accessories, woven baskets to hold logs and magazines, and dried grasses arranged in terra-cotta pitchers — furnishings that balance the glow of the colors with robust country practicality. This is a natural color scheme, despite its intensity and drama, so enjoy playing with the different shades until you get the precise effect you want.

○ Look at an autumn forest to get inspiration for your palette — collect leaves of different colors and press them to create a natural swatch board.

○ Mix different textures to reflect the variety of foliage — rough linens, soft velvets, chalky paint finishes, and twiggy baskets.

○ The Hay & Russet palette is rich enough not to need accenting, but you can cool it down with soft mushroom or offset the orangey red with a touch of contrasting green to represent a patch of summer foliage that hasn't yet turned.

○ Combine the two colors in a single colorwashed wall, layering russet on top of hay so that flashes of gold gleam through the darker surface.

Left: Warm colorwashed walls and yellow painted ceiling beams are toned down by wainscoting and a large striped throw in a cooler, mushroomy shade. (See page 28 for more advice on using these mushroom colors.)

Right: A stack of pillows in different textures and harvest colors blends with the polished surface of a carved chair back.

russet & mushroom

○ Add natural accessories such as baskets, dried grasses, and woven twig wreaths to tie in with the neutral mushroom tones.

○ Use soft mushroom to add muted accents to stronger colors without creating harsh contrasts.

○ Look for natural fabrics to carry the color — linens, muslin, burlap, and jute or coir floor coverings.

○ Mix different textures to give the limited palette more interest, adding rough-surfaced wood and including a few unglazed tiles among the glazed ones on a wall or counter.

The pinky beige of field mushrooms has a cool elegance that perfectly balances the bright, burnished shades of fall. Quiet and muted, it calms down the stronger colors, providing a neutral contrast far gentler than pure white. Whereas white details can be harsh and unforgiving, this soft taupe takes the heat out of warm russet, its subtle accents blending with the red tones rather than highlighting their difference.

To prevent the two shades from fighting, try to avoid using them in equal quantities where it's not clear which one has precedence. Use the russet for touches of robust color in a room with predominantly neutral tones, or the mushoom to add cooling touches to a wall painted in bold russet. And bring out the natural texture of the mushroom color by mixing different finishes such as loose linen weaves, hand-embroidered patterns, mother-of-pearl buttons, and glazed ceramic tiles.

Right: Warm russet takes the clinical chill off a bathroom and softens the strong lines of the timber beams, which could look stark against a paler color. Contrasting paintwork and ceramic tiles in a muted mushroom shade provide a gentle balance.

Below left: Russet-colored fabric scattered with faded flowerheads makes an elegant pillow cover when trimmed with a wide border of plain linen and a neat button fastening.

Below: This loose-fitting linen chair slipcover in pale mushroom has been embroidered with a flowing fern design to reinforce the natural hedgerow theme. The pillow adds a flash of brighter warmth to the faded color scheme.

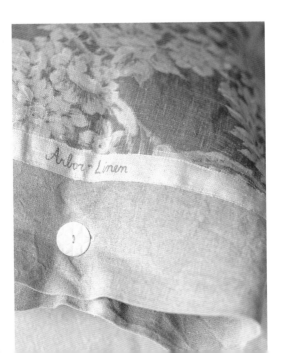

berry & holly

Startling and dramatic, the contrast of bright red and deep green has a refreshing boldness that can be used for very different effects, creating both elegant formality if combined with traditional furniture and practical country style created with simple fabrics and distressed paint finishes. The drama springs from the fact that the two shades respond to each other like opposites attracted. Why? Because each of the three primary colors has a natural pair in the color made by mixing the other two primaries together. This "complementary" color acts as both balance and highlighter. So green, which is mixed from blue and yellow, cools down the rich warmth of the red, and at the same time throws it into sharper relief. It's the crisp combination of bright winter berries against glossy evergreen leaves, appearing rich and jewel-like in a season when so much of the landscape is fading into neutral.

Right: The foreground room, painted in deep green, creates a striking contrast with the bold red walls of the room beyond. Soft white paintwork and graceful antique furniture and artifacts highlight the elegant architectural lines.

Below: Fresh red and white checked fabric and an old green-painted bench show the color combination in a simpler, less formal light, reflecting the natural leaf and berry associations of the two shades.

○ Play with the strong contrast of these complementary colors by using them in adjoining rooms to give the view greater depth.

○ Vary the effect by mixing them with polished wood and Regency stripes for formal elegance, or incorporating them in simple paintwork and gingham fabric for a more casual look.

○ Look for polished or burnished surfaces such as green or red leather chairs and desktops to recreate the glossy finish of leaves and berries.

○ Offset the rich colors with white paintwork to create the wintry look of frost on holly.

wheat, hay & meadow

Below: Old green enamel mellows the gold of this kitchen.

Below right: A softer yellow provides the background for painted green furniture and a natural linen-covered chair.

The greens and golds of the summer countryside are a joyous, life-affirming mixture that translates brilliantly into furnishing color schemes and provides surprising variety within its palette. The beauty of this combination is its sun-filled quality. Yellow, whether intense and glowing or pale and buttery, has an infectiously cheerful nature that lights up everything it touches, while the green of summer foliage and meadow grasses sounds a fresher, softer note. How you use the two colors depends on whether you want them to blend or contrast. Rich yellows, accented with touches of gilt in paintwork or picture frames, will work in harmony with mid-greens, especially if the green is used for a polished

surface such as glass or enamel so that it reflects the gleam of the gold. Soft yellows, like pale corn, will provide a gentle background for stronger, deeper greens without the two shades fighting for attention. Think of the way fields are edged by darker borders of hedgerow foliage. Layer contrasting greens and yellows together, offsetting their brightness with patches of cooler, neutral color — a solid-colored chair, a set of linen curtains — so that you introduce a sense of how they fade naturally in the countryside. These are warm, inviting shades that fill the gloomiest corner with sunshine, creating welcoming entry halls, light-reflecting sunrooms, and the sort of kitchen that everyone will want to spend time in.

○ Yellow is a strong color to work with, but if you mix different yellows together they will temper each other's character.

○ Introduce neutral mushroom and oatmeal shades to tone the yellows down further and calm the energy of the brighter shades.

○ To bring out the richer tones of the yellow, add touches of gilding such as ornamental mirror and picture frames, gold-leaf patterning on walls and furniture, or little gold-painted tables and chairs.

○ Include plenty of plants and foliage to add natural greenery to the layout and maintain a sense of growth and regeneration.

chestnut & copper beech

The woodland combination of textured bark, polished horse chestnuts, and burnished copper beech leaves is irresistibly deep and rich. Moodier than the bright fall shades, these colors have a more somber look that lifts them out of the traditionally rustic and lets you use them in starker, more contemporary settings, creating sleekly sophisticated effects. Nutshells and copper beech trees share a delightful quality of variegated color, providing subtly contrasting shades within their deep brown surfaces. In horse chestnuts, this can create a layered, almost colorwashed effect — as though they had been polished over the years like well-worn leather, smooth and glossy with some areas stained darker than others. On copper beech trees, the leaves themselves may change with startling splendor from mahogany to bright copper as the sap dwindles through summer and fall.

To make the most of the colors in this palette, let these shades provide their own natural contrasts

◯ Use textures to echo the effect of the colors — polished wood and leather contrasting with soft, tweedy throws and blankets.

◯ Use plaids and patterns for a more homey effect, and plain fabrics for elegance and drama.

◯ Accent the browns with yellows and ochers to create a warm, mellow setting, or with whites and grays to keep the look cool and sophisticated.

◯ Experiment with the palette, introducing "transitional" shades to the pure red and brown for a more informal look.

◯ Combine the warmest shades in living rooms and studies, or try a cooler mix for a relaxing bedroom.

Below left: Dark wood reinforces this room's mixed reds and browns.

Below: Polished wood glows against the brighter, coppery shade of the wall.

Below right: A flash of red adds instant drama to these neutral browns, whites, and grays.

among your furnishings. The direction you take depends on the proportions you use of each color, and the shades you pick to add the room's accents and highlights. The brighter, red-based tones will be a dramatic background for formal, polished furniture and gilt-framed pictures. Darker, more solid browns echo the beams and traditional woodwork of the rustic style, so you can emphasize this with unpainted doors and dark-stained floorboards. If you pick up the transitional shades in warm, textured fabrics such as plaids and blanket-weave, you

will continue the cottagey theme as well as provide contrast to the smoother surface of the wood; highlights of gold and yellow give the whole effect a mellow autumnal feel. For a completely different look, use touches of dark chestnut brown and flashes of brighter copper to accent a more neutral color scheme, and you have an altogether more contemporary style — crisp whites and muted grays are cool and wintry, and the introduction of a few layers of rich nut shades gives the room a sense of real drama.

moss & lichen

○ Use this soft, restrained palette to echo garden shades in muted tones, exchanging bright yellow leaf colors for nearly neutral greens.

○ Look for pale silvery green paints to maximize gentle light reflection and make small rooms feel larger and brighter.

○ Combine light and dark shades to create subtle contrasts and accent door frames and other woodwork.

These delicate shades are a godsend when you want color to be very subtle but not totally neutral. Whereas most pastels conjure up sherbet flavors or cottage-garden flowers, the organic character of green takes it closer to neutral creams, taupes, and grays — naturally muted yet still with its own distinctive color quality. Pale and elegant, soft greens set the tone for restful living rooms, tranquil bedrooms, and cool, Scandinavian-style dining rooms. Especially effective in rooms that overlook gardens, they reflect the haze of nearby foliage and bring a sense of the outdoor world inside. But this isn't the fresh, bright green of spring leaves — it's the subtle, silvery bloom you find where patches of lichen highlight textured bark and old stone walls combined with the deeper tones of gentle, velvety moss. Use the darker shades for mellow woodwork

as the backdrop to comfortable scroll-armed sofas and faded tapestry rugs. Make the most of the paler, light-reflective colors for painted wooden furniture in graceful shapes to recreate an elegant setting reminiscent of traditional Gustavian style, shifting to slightly darker, earthier shades with which to accent occasional pieces and architectural details.

The natural quality of this palette makes it easy to adapt to many styles — from old-fashioned florals to simple country patterns — so you can transform your look totally by incorporating different fabrics into the design. Use chintzy pink roses and trailing foliage for a traditional country-house living room; or Shaker-style checks in gray-greens for a simpler study or breakfast room, echoed by arrangements of lavender, rosemary, and eucalyptus leaves.

Above: The bright green checked shade echoes the foliage outside and illuminates the more muted gray-green of the wainscoting.

Left: Subdued moss green paintwork contrasts with the paler walls of this living room and picks out the foliage in the faded fabrics and carpets.

Right: Walls and furniture painted in shades of soft, silvery lichen are accented by deeper gray-green accents and the dark blue-green of decorative foliage.

cornfield & plowed earth

The pale gold of summer cornfields is a fabulous background for country furnishings — warm and sunny, but not too aggressively yellow. Combine it with somber earthy browns and dark wood, and you recreate the contrast of adjacent fields, some thick with corn, others plowed into stripes of newly turned earth. Rough-textured wood and uneven beams carry these darker colors very eloquently, while the paler yellow can turn up in the muted shades of flaking stonework and fading limewashed walls.

To make the most of the cornfield theme, look for chunky, rustic-style furniture that reinforces the sense of the country as a working environment, such as solid, artisan-made square chests and tables and plain plank doors with blacksmith-forged latches and hinges. Or give the colors a more elegant interpretation by translating them into lighter, more graceful painted furniture and miniature pieces decorated with stenciled details or delicate marquetry patterns. These daintier designs are perfect for introducing woods and veneers with paler finishes and intriguing grains — like walnut, burl elm, and fruitwoods — and for showing off ornamental surfaces such as the age-distressed effect of craquelure. Whereas robust furnishings go best with simple coir matting and rush-seated chairs, you can combine elegant little carved side tables and wooden chairs with pretty needlepoint and embroidered fabrics in faded colors.

Left: The classic country colors of pale corn, plowed fields, and textured bark translate naturally into mellow designs with rough-plastered walls, uneven beams, and chunky unfinished wood furniture.

Right: The same shades create a more delicate effect when used for painted wood and elegant marquetry patterns.

○ Yellow paint shades can be tricky to get right, so try to find unusual surfaces that provide natural pale yellow tones, such as old flagstone floors and rush matting.

○ Accent the yellows and browns with touches of coppery red. Think of the richer tones of clay soil and introduce them in pictures and accessories.

○ In simpler, more rustic settings you can echo the natural color scheme with a jug of dried grasses or tall, dark-tipped bulrushes. If you opt for a more elegant furnishing style, try pretty meadow flowers, mixing in a few contrasting shades among the yellow.

○ The beauty of this palette is its natural quality, so echo the earthy, mellow tones with distressed or weathered surfaces that look as though they've seen plenty of use.

SUN, SEA & SKY

SUN, SEA & SKY

THE SEASHORE HAS ITS OWN UNIQUE CHARACTER. Of all the impressions evoked by country settings, this is the place that creates the most vivid memories of warmth and relaxation, suggesting summer and freedom, far horizons and unbroken sky. It has long been a source of materials and inspiration for decorating houses. Nautical-striped fabrics, plain sailcloth, and curtains lashed with rope or cord lend rooms a practical, functional feel. Model boats and lighthouses provide cheerful decoration for bathrooms and children's rooms. The soft, weathered honeys and grays of driftwood make attractive picture and mirror frames, while sea-polished pebbles and pearlescent shells have a natural beauty that has graced innumerable display shelves and dressing tables. This chapter explores all the subtle variations of tone and texture associated with seaside colors. The sea itself provides a palette incorporating greens, grays, and blues of all shades, from the palest translucent aquamarine to deep inky blue-black. Pink and golden sand, bleached white chalk, rainbow pebbles, and purple mudflats are set against a range of sky shades, from pure cerulean blue to the rose and coral streaks that pierce the sky when the sun is setting to the deep pewter of heavy storm clouds.

Right: The contrasting colors of the seashore include the pale blue of summer skies, bright red of sand toys and striped beach umbrellas. Cheerful and practical, these are shades that mix happily together and conjure up a relaxed mood of freedom and vacations.

THE SUN, SEA & SKY PALETTE

These ten shades provide a basic palette for recreating the natural colors of the shoreline. Concentrate on cool blues and aquas to conjure up a fresh, watery feel, or head for the yellows and pinks if you want warmer, sunnier tones. Mixing the two together will create bright, energetic contrasts and a very summery look, while introducing subtler shades of gray and off-white will calm the effect down and provide a softer, more restful setting. Let this palette inspire your initial color scheme, then draw in other variations from the combinations shown on the following pages.

chalk

A cool, powdery white that provides clean, fresh accents against blues, greens, and yellows and creates a neutral background without the harsh glare sometimes associated with brighter whites. It works particularly well on uneven or textured surfaces such as rough-plastered walls and wood paneling, which bring out its chalky highlights.

coral

A glowing pink that adds a warmer tinge to cool seaside blues and greens, and introduces a touch of unexpected color to the palette. Reminiscent of shells and the sky at sunset, it has a softer, prettier feel, more like the Flowers & Blossom palette, and enables you to create more varied effects than the fresh, watery tones of the Sun, Sea & Sky palette usually permit.

sand

The pale yellow of childhood vacation beaches, warm but not overpoweringly hot, so that at its softest it is almost neutral. Sand is an excellent background color for living areas, where it is comfortable and inviting without making too strong a statement. It also mixes beautifully with most blues and contains just enough yellow to throw whites and creams into sharp contrast.

sunshine

A brighter, hotter yellow, with a stimulating, energetic quality. Cheerful and glowing, this is a color that really warms things up. It is a brilliant alternative to sunlight in small-windowed or north-facing rooms that don't get much natural illumination. It's not remotely subtle but can be great fun to use. Try it in the kitchen or playroom or to take the chill out of a gloomy bathroom.

aqua

A wonderfully soothing, refreshing color, perfect for bathrooms and bedrooms. So pale that it's almost translucent, aqua has a light-reflective quality that means it is an excellent space-maker, good for opening up small rooms. The cool, watery tone provides an intriguing contrast both with warm sunny yellows and with the rosier, pink-tinged colors of coral and coastal flowers.

sky blue

A perennial favorite for kitchens and bathrooms. Light and clear, it's almost endlessly usable — a safe choice and very easy to live with. The perfect wall color to cool down over-bright rooms, sky blue is also a good space-maker and creates fresh, uncomplicated combinations with yellows, greens, pinks, and deeper, stronger blues.

rockpool

A subtle alternative to the luminous glow of aqua. This gray-green shade has something of the muted practicality of traditional Shaker colors, although its character is liquid rather than earthy. Mix it with blues, grays, aquas, and chalk white, letting its cool, intangible quality add depth and interest to the purer colors in this palette.

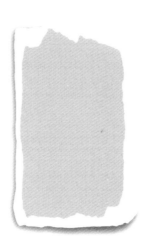
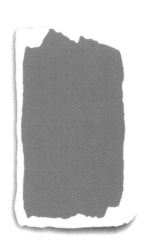

caribbean bay

Bright and dramatic — a color that makes an instant impact and never lets you forget it's there. It's not for the faint-hearted, but is highly energizing if you have the courage to use it and is a brilliant way to conjure up atmosphere. Vibrant and slightly exotic, it pushes the natural shades of sun, sea, and sky to their most extreme, so that you can almost feel the tropical heat.

azure

A warmer, richer blue for when you want stronger contrasts or a brighter background. This is the shade that can hold its own against dramatic Caribbean colors, as well as create bold accents against glowing sunny yellows. Fresh and lively, it has a simple quality that feels practical enough to use in kitchens and children's rooms.

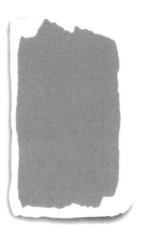
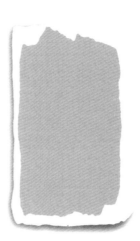

storm

The deeper tone that emerges when the blues of sky and sea lose their sparkle. Moody and cool, this adds stronger accents and lets you vary the pace of the brighter, fresher colors. It can supply drama where you need it, but it also has a neutral tranquility and a close affinity with the pale green of sea and rockpools, making it a soothing contrast to bold blues and yellows.

Left: Sunshine streams down this yellow-painted hallway, reflected by the walls and cooled by the soft gray-blue of the woodwork. Bold striped rugs and a wood floor add a practical, nautical air.

Above: Clear sky blue creates a background for brighter, Caribbean-style turquoise tableware and sunshine-yellow flowers in this simple dining room.

Above right: The colorwashed finish of the walls gives them a faded, sun-bleached look, which is matched by the driftwood effect of the old weathered beams. Touches of blue add contrast.

Right: Sea green is cool and restful enough to employ in abundance — here it is used for the paneled wall as well as the painted chairs and striped curtains.

Far left: The huge mop-heads of pale green guelder roses seem almost translucent against a background of blue-painted paneling, with touches of bright aqua and azure adding highlights.

Middle left: This pair of painted wooden chairs is chalk white against a wall of very pale sand and the sky-blue door. A clutch of yellow narcissi adds a burst of sunshine.

Left: The colors of white cotton clouds in a blue summer sky are perfect for the paintwork and tiles of this little bathroom. The cool and refreshing design is accented with a grass-green towel rack.

Below left: Deeper blues and greens create the moodier feel of the sea at night or in stormy weather, with the dark gray of the floor adding somber shadows.

Below: Clear blue walls have a classic elegance, here stippled to give a watery, colorwashed effect. Cool and light-reflective, they are the perfect background for the mellow stone fireplace.

Far left: Cheerful checks and stripes conjure up the simple practicality of seaside style as well as its colors. White-painted paneling continues the beachhouse theme, with little colored lanterns providing a decorative version of traditional nautical lighting.

Left: Use seaside memorabilia and beachcombing finds to reinforce the theme. Little painted boats are perfect decoration for bathrooms and children's rooms, with shells, starfish, and even dried seaweed strands providing unusual accessories.

Below left: Seaside colors work just as well in inland country settings. Use a pale sandy background for a gentle, restful atmosphere, adding painted blue-green woodwork and fabrics in subtle shades of pebble and driftwood.

Right: The combination of bleached wood and painted paneling is instantly ship-shape, with drawstring bags adding neat nautical storage on their practical peg rail.

sky & sunshine

The brightest of the seaside color schemes is also one of the most irresistible, rich with childhood memories of how summer ought to be. Perhaps the sun wasn't always that bright, or the sky so cloudlessly blue, but this joyous combination will make up for it, flooding rooms with sunlight and creating a sense of instant vacation. It's the simplicity that makes it such a good plan for children's rooms: bright and stimulating, and with shades that seem perfect in simple fabric patterns like gingham checks and candy stripes. But it's well suited to the rest of the house too: cheerful and welcoming in an entry hall, merry and fresh in a living room. The only thing you need to watch is the balance between the two shades. Think about which one is going to be your major color, because this will establish the mood of the room. A predominantly yellow background with touches of blue will be warm and restful; reverse that with a blue-painted room furnished with flashes of yellow, and the atmosphere becomes cooler and fresher. White accents will offset either design with clean, crisp highlights, so aim for white woodwork and simple, white-painted furniture. A few pieces of natural wood and stone can be used to soften the sharp contrasts if needed.

○ It's hard to go wrong with blue and yellow, so use the colors with confidence and let the sunny combination add freshness and light.

○ Look for simple fabric patterns that reflect the practical colors. Nautical stripes combine well with graphic checks and solid-colored cottons.

○ Use the color combination in kitchens, children's rooms, sun-filled living rooms, and chilly bathrooms.

○ Add splashes of different colors for accessories and other details.

Far left: This gentle, sunny wall is warm and glowing against the pale sky-blue paintwork of the door. Splashes of beachball red in flowers and accessories brighten up the setting.

Left: Yellow checked fabrics add zesty freshness to this little blue sitting room, offsetting the cooler, crisp-colored walls.

Right: A yellow rose and natural pebble tones warm up the cool sky blue of the wall.

chalk & sky

The fresh, crisp mix of blue and white is a classic color scheme. Though especially appropriate for kitchens and bathrooms, it is perfect almost everywhere, from practical children's rooms to country living rooms to elegant dining room china cabinets. At its simplest, pale sky blue looks completely at home on painted woodwork, where the natural shadows of paneling and door frames coax tonal depth out of a single color. Used in this way, this shade acquires deeper accents of gray and ultramarine, while chalk white lends itself particularly well to broken or distressed paintwork that highlights the powdery quality of its color. Try plain whitewashed or pickled wood, too, to create a similar effect of weathering or sun-bleaching. Painted floors and furniture respond well to these shades, and clapboard siding can be painted blue for an instant seaside feel. This simple combination barely needs accessorizing with other colors, but clean reds, pinks, and yellows will all add beach-bright accents, and touches of fresh green are reminiscent of a stretch of clifftop grass separating cliffs and sky.

Left: Blue painted clapboard siding and flaking white woodwork create the sky and chalk mix at this beachside house. The pebbles and bright flowerheads add warmer tones of gold and coral.

Right: The white-painted armoire and chair create a crisp contrast with their blue background. The simple color scheme effectively highlights the accents of the woodwork, from the plank floor to the carved detailing around the top of the armoire.

❍ Take inspiration from the way mismatched blue and white china mixes on a kitchen hutch — the different shades and patterns blend together because of the white background and glazed surfaces that they have in common.

❍ Add warmer neutrals and natural accessories to offset the chill of the main colors. Pebbles, shells, basketware, and coir matting all work well.

❍ Use painted wood furniture if possible. Any natural wood should be pale, stripped, bleached, or pickled — aim for the soft, textured effect of driftwood rather than dark, polished surfaces.

aqua & azure

If you had any lingering doubts about the wisdom of using blue and green together, these clear, liquid colors are the ones to change your mind. Shades of sky, from the pale blue of very early morning to the bright, cloudless expanse of high summer, blend beautifully with turquoise and aqua greens. Gentle and luminous, they work particularly well in soft paint finishes — think of the slight sheen on furniture or paneling painted in eggshell catching the light like sun on water, while faded colorwashed effects reflect both the translucence of water and the heat of the sun. Layer close shades of blue and green on top of one another and enjoy the tranquility of their cool, refreshing harmony.

Left: Faded blue paintwork gives a sun-bleached look to the paneling and chair, while the door and floorboards are painted a brighter, fresher shade of aqua green.

Below left: Wooden coathangers and other practical accessories painted in cool, watery colors create gentle contrasts and provide a chance to try out different toning shades.

Below right: Polkadot fabrics, ceramics, and wallpaper pick out the different shades of blue and echo the simplicity of the color scheme. The painted cabinet adds a note of translucent liquid green.

○ **Use aqua and azure in kitchens and bathrooms, rooms whose natural associations with water link them inherently to these cool, refreshing colors.**

○ Keep the colors pale and liquid so the contrasts are gentle and the shades blend into one another as though dissolving in water.

○ Look for light-reflective or broken-color surfaces that complement the sense of delicate, intangible color. Distressed or colorwashed paintwork suggest bleaching by the sun or weathering from sea spray. Materials like old-fashioned enamel and lusterware have an iridescent finish that catches and diffuses light.

○ Keep patterns understated. Striped towels and curtains can be echoed by the lines of simple wood paneling and plank doors on cabinets, giving a traditional beachhouse feel.

61

rockpool & driftwood

The subtlest of all the coastal colors are the gray-greens that emerge when the sun is fading: the muted shades of shallow water that captures the last of the dwindling light and reveals the shadows of rocks and billowing seaweed beneath its surface. At their purest, these colors have the translucence of limestone rockpools, where the clear white of the stone shows through the water and intensifies its color. Cool and still, these tranquil hues have something of the same effect as the Moss & Lichen shades shown on page 36 — they are so pale that they're almost neutral, but with just enough tone to provide their own character. Restful as a background, with deeper accents supplying essential line and definition, these colors are easy to use and comfortable to live with — the perfect decorating combination.

To emphasize their natural quality, mix them with pickled or bleached wood furniture and picture frames — faded surfaces reminiscent of shoreline driftwood and salt-whitened clapboard siding. These gentle neutrals blend beautifully with pale greens, grays, and blues, creating mellow color schemes for rooms you will relax in.

Below left: Simple watercolor paintings in hazy shades of gray and green explore the subtleties of the rockpool palette. The brighter wood of the old printer's trays emphasizes just how muted the background colors are.

Right: The faded wooden frame of a director's chair sits alongside more colorful painted designs. The pale green is a gentle background for a collection of old pictures.

○ Use these shades as background colors, letting their soft, light-reflective quality provide restful calm.

○ Add furniture and accessories in darker greens and harmonious blues to bring out their deeper tones and create gentle contrast.

○ Add touches of brighter blue for sparkle — as though sunshine were highlighting these areas of the room.

○ Use chalk whites for occasional clean accents so that the gray tones don't look muddy.

○ For moodier accents, add purply grays — the color of mudflats, mussel shells, and sea-washed pebbles.

caribbean seascape

The most intense shades of blue and green have a vivid, vibrant character that is saturated with color. These are the sun-soaked shades of Caribbean beaches — colors that are generally too exotic for everyday use, but provide flashes of brilliance in unexpected places and a glorious way to enliven individual rooms and dark corners. In a bedroom, try the intense turquoise green of the Caribbean sea; it will glow extra-deep when lamplit by night, and will become almost translucent in the morning sun. Use the rich blue of a tropical night sky to turn an entry hall into a room in its own right.

Right: The deep blue of an evening sky, shot with lighter hues as though glowing in the moonlight, is cool and mysterious, a dramatic contrast against the bright green paintwork of the window seat.

Below: Bright aqua floods an entire room with color so that it bounces off the wall and cupboard and tints the softer shades of the pictures and the painted chair.

○ It takes courage to use these bolder shades, but the risk is worth taking — after using them, you'll never be frightened of color again.

○ Try these shades in nighttime rooms — living rooms used for evening entertaining, dining rooms, and bedrooms — where they respond particularly well to atmosphere and candlelight.

○ Match their intense shades with splashes of accent color or painted furniture in bright parrot reds and yellows: a scarlet vase or zesty lemon pillow will maintain the tropical vacation feel.

○ For a mellower look, add weathered terra-cotta, the flaking, faded surface of which provides a textured contrast with the rich colors.

shell, sky, & sunset

○ This is the palette where the colors of the seaside overlap with those of the flowerbed, so it gives you a chance to introduce softer, prettier elements.

○ Pink provides a third primary color but in diluted form, offsetting blues and yellows with a softer shade than bright red.

○ Touches of pink and coral warm up blues and enrich yellows, or even make a simple blue background sharp and contemporary.

○ Introduce shades of pink in accessories, so that they don't dominate the setting or detract from the freshness of a blue or yellow scheme.

○ Look for authentic materials that emphasize the quality of the colors: pinks and whites in iridescent surfaces such as lusterware and mother-of pearl, blues and yellows in chalky Mediterranean paints.

The traditional blues and yellows of the coast take on a new character if you work pink into the mixture, reflecting the pretty shades of shell and coral, the warm glow of a setting sun, and, in brighter flashes, the vivid pinks of seaside flowers like thrift and tamarisk. At its simplest, this can mean setting a vase of pink blooms against a blue wall, but to integrate the colors more completely you could look for a fabric that incorporates pink with the traditional combination of blue and yellow in its pattern, or accessorize a predominantly blue and yellow room with pillows, rugs, or china in shell pink. Weathered pink paintwork and raw plastered walls evoke the layered, streaked effect of a sunset sky, and pale terra-cotta tiles echo the soft pinky beige of sea-washed pebbles.

Left: Walls half-painted in a chalky terra-cotta shade add a glowing warmth to this yellow kitchen with its sky-blue woodwork.

Below: Flashes of deep pink, like blooms of thrift or the waving tentacles of sea anemones, are bold and dramatic against traditional blue-painted beachhouse paneling.

storm cloud & sea spray

○ Look for natural materials in the colors — a dish of gray and white pebbles on a windowsill, a slab of marble on a white-painted washstand, slate floors and counters, and alabaster vases.

○ Monitor the level of color carefully — don't let it get too blue or too green or you will lose the subtle anonymity of this intangible shade.

○ Keep the color scheme alive with plenty of fresh white accents, or the moody, somber tone may start to feel oppressive.

○ Use it in bright, south-facing rooms that get plenty of sun and need calming down. These cooler tones will make the space more comfortable.

The sea has its darker moods, and the pewter gray of a threatening storm adds somber color that anchors light, fresh decorating designs and gives them more impact. Reflecting hints of sea green and sky blue in its shadowy tone, storm cloud provides a coolly dramatic background for painted furniture, pretty fabrics, and displayed paintings. Use it with plenty of white, like the frothy waves of a storm-tossed sea, and the effect is fresh and distinctive, the crisp contrast insuring that the muted gray never becomes gloomy.

This is a color scheme just made for bathrooms and kitchens, where it gives paintwork and paneling a simple, functional look. It is also effective in bedrooms, where its lack of obvious color is quietly soothing, as though the light had been switched off to calm down the energetic glare of the sun. Choose your shade of storm cloud or sea spray carefully, and it will have the stillness of Wedgwood blue, producing a deep, subtle background against which white paintwork and accents stand out like the classic cameos and silhouettes on a Wedgwood vase.

Left: Cool gray paintwork gives this bathroom a practical finish, calming down the brighter cobalt blue of the floor and echoing the darker touches of inky blue in the ceramics and shower curtain.

Right: A moody gray wall provides a dramatic background under the eaves of this attic bedroom, contrasting with the sloping white walls and pretty floral bedlinen.

○ Use these subtle, muted colors in simple, Shaker-style kitchens, as well as in living rooms — their quiet character makes them easy to live with.

○ Maintain the mellow feel of the room by opting for plain wood and natural floor coverings.

○ Add simple accessories and naive-style paintings that suit the faded colors and evoke childhood memories.

○ If you're worried about the colors starting to seem muddy, freshen the scheme by adding touches of white and cream.

sand &
summer sky

The pale gold of a sandy beach — almost white when dry and bleached, darker where the tide has drenched it — brings back memories of childhood visits to the coast. You can almost feel the grains between your toes, your feet shifting their hold as the water is squeezed out beneath them. Chalky, Mediterranean paint finishes recapture that texture, as do pigment-mixed limewashes, with color that fades and surges in response to the amount of moisture in the walls. Best of all, it's a mellow, earthy color that's restful to live with — richer than cream but still softer than the bright cheerfulness of sunshine yellow. Combine it with the blue of old painted boats, children's beach buckets, and vintage postcard skies, and you end up with a nostalgic scheme that's all the more evocative for its faded quality, as though it's been weathered by use. Not as bright or fresh as the Sky & Sunshine combination, it has strong resemblances to the muted tones of Shaker style and suits the same understated lines: simple furniture, painted floorboards, and plain woodwork reminiscent of nautical decking.

Left: Simple Shaker lines give this living room a restrained, old-fashioned look, with muddy-blue paintwork and plain wood against whitewashed floorboards and pale, sand-colored walls.

Right: Old enamel storage jars and plain checked curtains in a soft, muted blue add nostalgic color against pale yellow walls.

FLOWERS & BLOSSOM

FLOWERS & BLOSSOM

THIS PASTEL PALETTE provides endless inspiration, with soft, sweet shades. Because of their similarity in tone, they can be intermingled in almost any combination without jarring — from the mixed rainbow of sweet peas to self-contained combinations such as pink tulip heads tinged with cream. Whether in fabric, wallpaper, or paint colors, these blues, pinks, creams, and mauves, juxtaposed with the pale green of summer foliage, conjure up the beauty of country gardens and cottage borders. Saturated with summer memories, the flowers suggest intriguing textures too, the contrasts between frothy blossom, velvety rose petals, tight-wrapped buds, and frilly pinked carnation heads providing the sort of variety you need in furnishings and finishes. Overlapping occasionally with Sun, Sea & Sky shades and with the prettier end of the Kitchen Garden palette, they can be shot through with subtle highlights and will shift and change during their life. Hydrangeas can start off one color and end up another; bright blue forget-me-nots can be flecked with pink; scarlet rosebuds streaked with yellow may become the palest pink when open. Full of surprises, never predictable, flowers also acquire a silvery pearlescence from early morning frost and dew, so look for enamel, mother-of-pearl, and shimmering satins to add luster to the color.

Right: Fragile rose petals in soft pink tinged with gold represent the delicacy of the colors and textures of flowers found in country garden borders.

THE FLOWERS & BLOSSOM PALETTE

These ten shades provide a basic palette for recreating a gardenful of floral furnishing colors. Use the paler, pastel blues, pinks, and mauves to devise restful, romantic designs in bedrooms and living rooms, then add brighter, crisper accents with energetic spring hues and touches of rich luxury with deep pinks, reds, and purples. Incorporate plenty of fresh greens to supply an element of cool, leafy calm, and enjoy experimenting with these harmonious, nostalgic shades. Let this palette inspire your initial color scheme, then draw in other variations on the same theme from the combinations shown on the following pages.

primrose

The pale yellow that appears in spring drifts along woodland banks and in shady gardens. Incredibly delicate, it's barely more than cream; its pure shade comes through only when used in quantity as a wall color, or when highlighted by contrasting accents of pink or purple. Take a look at the Kitchen Garden palette (page 106) to find similar soft, milky shades.

alchemilla

A soft, yellowy green that can sometimes appear as one color, sometimes as the other, depending on the accents with which you offset it. Fresh and cool, it works especially well in natural sunlight and has a glowing, reflective quality. Try using it with pale mauves so that it echoes the traditional cottage garden combination of lady's mantle (alchemilla) and lavender.

cherry blossom

The pale pink that smothers trees in spring — very soft and versatile and not too sugary. An incredibly gentle, restful shade, it is traditionally used for babies' bedrooms but is equally suitable for bathrooms, living rooms, and anywhere that you want a hint of warmth without feeling overwhelmed by color. If you've never thought of yourself as a "pink" person, this is the one to try.

lilac

A soft hazy shade, almost gray but with a pretty pastel tint to it. Beautifully tranquil and light-reflective, the color of lilac blossom is fresh but soothing, its cool, calming nature creating the perfect background for bedrooms, bathrooms, and living rooms. A distinctive alternative to blues and pinks, it mixes comfortably with the yellows and greens of the spring garden.

sweet pea

A full, strong pink that can hold its own against the dark purples and fuchsias of a mixed summer flowerbed. The fragility of the sweet-pea petals doesn't dilute this color, so it is an extraordinary combination of vibrance and delicacy. It takes more courage to use, but is wonderful with fresh leafy greens and soft, creamy yellows, which cool down its lively tones.

peony

The deep color of the traditional garden peony. A bold shade that hovers between red and pink, it is also found in the crimson-flushed tips of the softer, paler pink peony and in velvety, scented roses. Strong but not harsh, it's surprisingly easy to live with, adding rich, luxurious accents and mixing well with both floral pastels and earthier, faded colors.

forget-me-not

A clean, clear blue, cool as ice but full of summer sunshine. The classic shade for kitchens, bathrooms, and baby boys' bedrooms, it also offers a refreshing way of toning down rooms that feel too bright. It has an intense quality despite its pastel paleness — the flowers glow from leafy flowerbeds like pinpricks of light. This translucence means the color is a brilliant space-maker for small rooms.

bluebell

The purply blue that appears in spring and continues through summer in flowers such as grape hyacinth and agapanthus. Mauve in some lights, definitely blue in others, it is a shifting, intangible color that fades gradually through a range of shades and blends beautifully with most blues and lilacs.

leaf

Much stronger and brighter than alchemilla, but still contributing a light, yellow tone that always feels spring-like. Fresh and energetic, it mixes comfortably with all the floral shades, but can also be used with the deeper, mellower greens of the Kitchen Garden (page 106) or to add a zesty crispness to the golds and russets of the Field & Woodland palette (page 18).

violet

Darker and moodier than lilac, and capable of more dramatic effects. Violet has the pretty coloring of the rest of the floral palette, but its deeper tones are more robust in comparison with the delicate pastels. Use it to create opulence and atmosphere and mix it with gilded accessories for a sense of luxury. If you feel wary of such a strong shade, try it out in small accents.

Left: Bunches of lilac, lavender, and heather are hung upside down to air-dry in a rustic powder room. Green-painted tips on the old-fashioned peg rail echo the colors of the foliage.

Right: Bluebells are the stuff of fairytales — in folk legend, a child who picked them alone in the wood would never be seen again. These woodland flowers, which flourish in secluded, shady gardens, hold a lovely range of blue and mauve colors in their delicate bells.

Far right: Cool lilac and fresh forget-me-not blue are pretty and restful in a white-painted bedroom, with touches of cherry blossom pink adding a contrasting trim to the bed's drapery.

Below: The pinks and greens of a summer garden will inspire a host of paint colors, fabrics, and accessories once you let your imagination loose.

Far left: Curtains patterned with moody violet flowers on a soft primrose background provide a dramatic flourish against a lighter, hazier, lilac-painted wall.

Left: Flower shades always work comfortably together because even the strongest colors are often mixed in vases and borders. Here, wild bluebells and deep pink tulips create a romantic, cottage garden pairing.

Below left: Greens are a natural partner for floral colors, recalling the foliage that surrounds them in garden, meadow, or woodland settings. The combination of green and purple is especially subtle, like borders of alchemilla and lavender spilling onto a cottage path.

Right: Neutral tones can be introduced to the floral mix too, a reminder that the blooms and foliage will gradually lose their color and fade to pale gold and bleached straw.

Far left: Decorative paintwork gives you the chance to incorporate a range of complementary shades in a single room. These freehand designs, loosely worked on a backdrop of simple wooden paneling, combine stylized flowers and leaves with more graphic, abstract shapes, mixing greens, blues, yellows, pinks, and lilacs in a pastel, summery haze.

Above left: Outdoor color schemes can reflect garden shades too, with simple contrasts picking up colors of flowers and foliage, as in this soft green-painted window frame against the chalky lilac wall of the house.

Above: The same combination of soft pinks and greens is carried through to the bedroom, with touches of crisp white linen to add subtle contrast.

Left: The smallest accessories will carry a color scheme through to the last detail. For instance, a bathroom decorated in flower shades has a wide range of possibilities — from soft pastel paints to pretty towels and floral-patterned fabrics and wallpapers. Even the soaps and toiletries can be chosen to match.

forget-me-not & cherry blossom

The clear ice color of forget-me-nots has a brighter quality than so many garden blues — pale but intense, so that they sparkle like clusters of pastel stars among the spring foliage. These tiny flowers, so simple and sure of themselves, spread unbelievably quickly and have a habit of turning pink in unexpected patches. Forget-me-not has the same simplicity of tone as its sister pastel, cherry blossom pink, which is why these two colors have provided the basis for generations of nursery furnishings — the traditional blue-for-a-boy, pink-for-a-girl mantra reflecting their uncomplicated nature. But their pure, gentle shades are equally restful when used in grown-ups' bedrooms and in bathrooms and living rooms, where their straightforward prettiness has an easy, undiluted charm. Soft cashmere blankets and beribboned satin quilts provide this sweetest of combinations with plenty of contrasting texture, while light, floaty voile or organza curtains add a more whimsical, romantic touch. Small-scale floral prints and patterns incorporating boughs of cherry blossom are perfect for these settings and will also mix effortlessly with simple country checks and stripes, especially if you trim them with pretty bows, rosettes, and delicate fabrics such as lace and eyelet. Be careful to keep the overall effect understated, however, with plenty of areas of plain color and crisp whites or soft creams to offset the pastels and prevent them from looking too sugary. Plain floorboards and light wood or painted furniture will reinforce the natural, unsophisticated feel of this color combination.

○ If you want to add more depth of color, introduce accents of lilac or slightly brighter sweet-pea shades.

○ Avoid using strong patterns that swamp the delicacy of the colors or fight with their purity. Keep it simple.

○ Vary the look of the room with natural wood for a rustic feel or painted furniture and floorboards for a prettier, daintier look.

Far left: Pastel blue bed coverings and pink checked curtains create a tranquil bedroom. The pillows covered in old-fashioned blankets striped in faded pinks and lilacs and simple secondhand furniture keep the effect practical rather than whimsical.

Left: Forget-me-not blue walls are matched by a blossom-pink blanket and soft quilts in deeper sweet-pea pastels.

Right: Ribbon ties add a pretty finish to a pink pillow placed on a blue-painted garden chair.

lilac & primrose

The sweet, pastel nature of some floral shades makes them look good enough to eat, and yellows and mauves are among the most delicious-looking, evoking the colors of candied almonds and little iced rosettes found on old-fashioned cookies and handmade Easter eggs. The color of scented blooms — lilac, lavender, violets, wild thyme — is powerfully atmospheric and adds a wistful, slightly mysterious effect to decorating schemes. But combine lilac with fresh, merry yellow — whether pale, delicate primrose, or the brighter gold of spring daffodils — and the mix is a heady one, full of interesting contrasts. The natural balance of warm yellow with cool lilac means they offset one another perfectly, tempering each other's strengths while at the same time the essential character of each color becomes more intense by their pairing. Try them together in a bedroom, where the combination of tranquil lilac to lull you to sleep and glowing yellow to wake you up creates the perfect blend. Or experiment with slightly stronger shades in a living room, setting deep amethyst glassware against a yellow wall, or finding a fabric that entwines the two.

○ Think of the combination of violets and primroses in Easter posies, and don't be afraid of using the two colors together. Shades of purple, mixed from the primary colors of blue and red, are natural partners to yellow, the third primary color, and will cool it down.

○ If the combination feels too strong, try it in a milder, less dramatic form by softening lilac into gray or yellow into cream. You will still have the warm–cool balance of colors.

○ Don't feel you have to mix large areas of solid color. A lilac pillow on a yellow sofa provides an effective accent, and a single fabric will happily combine floral sprigs in both shades.

○ If you let the colors get darker and moodier, you will still have an effective combination, but you will lose the fresh, spring appeal of the lighter shades.

Left: Painted on the upper and lower halves of a bedroom wall, the two contrasting colors balance one another, with paler gold and gray echoing their tones in the fabric of the chair.

Right: A bowl of creamy-yellow wild-chervil heads mixed with a few Canterbury bells sits next to an elegant lilac-banded tureen on this gingham tablecloth.

mixed hydrangeas

The shifting, unpredictable shades of old-fashioned hydrangea blooms are a true grab bag of decorating color. Opening out from their multiple buds into petals of pale, creamy green, they gradually flood with color. But even then you can't be sure what color will eventually dominate. The most likely is a strong, rosy pink, or perhaps a darker carmine red. The petals of certain types turn a clear sky blue — but only if planted in acid soil; if the soil is too alkaline, the blue gives way to pink again. You'll also find creamy white varieties in gardens, and store-bought blooms give you even more choice, including deep mauve shades. You don't often see different colored hydrangeas growing together in a domestic garden because the soil dictates the hydrangeas' color, but their sweet, intense shades have a natural affinity.

Draw inspiration not just from the colors but also from the shape of the blooms, and from the contrast between big pompom mop-head hydrangeas and the more delicate, feathery lace-cap varieties, which have a central filigree of tiny blossoms within their circle of larger flowers. Select different textures and patterns to reflect this variety — for example, setting soft, fluffy fabrics against intricate lace designs and wrought-iron decoration.

Far left: The painted surfaces of brickwork, furniture, and floorboards combine to create an interior-style floral color scheme on this outdoor terrace.

Left: A stack of soft blankets and satin pillowcases in hydrangea shades of pink and blue is accented by a vase of deeper purple blooms.

❍ Remember how hydrangea colors shift and fade, and keep your decorating plans flexible. You can add or subtract any of these shades if you want to make subtle changes to your design.

❍ Use the pale green of the early petals and the lace-cap buds to provide gentle accents and highlights in contrast to all the heady pinks and blues.

❍ The old-fashioned, romantic colors of these flowers makes them perfect use in for bedrooms and living rooms.

bluebell & lilac

For a few weeks each year, the garden hovers between spring and summer, and the drifts of bluebells give way to early blooms of scented lilac. Hazy and mutable, the colors of both flowers are hard to pinpoint, however well we think we know them, and however widespread their use has become as identifying nametags for specific shades. Bluebells can be pink or white as well as blue, and lilac comes in a range of hues from white through pinks, mauves, and reds to deepest purple. The clear blue and soft mauve varieties are the most familiar, and these are the colors that are easiest to live with, but even in these gentle shades you can see different tones providing depth and highlights. The blue fades from its initial spring intensity to a paler, luminous color; the mauve blossom holds deeper shadows within its bell-like clusters. Together these delicate colors, so similar in tone, create a combination of perfect freshness and tranquility, mixing quietly in fabrics and decorating plans that reflect their sweetness and bring a sense of the garden inside.

Left: The luminous blue of fading bluebells highlights the pretty decoration of this wrought-iron bed against the hazy, lilac-painted wall.

Right: The blues and mauves of these familiar garden blooms are mixed with harmonious pinks and touches of spring yellow. Soft white paintwork keeps the whole effect fresh and delicate.

❍ Aim for similarity of tone, adding other harmonious pastels rather than strongly contrasting colors.

❍ Look for small-scale floral patterns featuring these flowers, and mix them with solid colors and checks for a simple, country-garden effect.

❍ Keep the furniture light and elegant, with pale paintwork and graceful shapes such as carved wood and decorative wrought iron.

❍ Add traditional accessories to match the old-fashioned colors — crystal chandeliers, dainty ceramics, scallop-edged lampshades, and vintage patchwork quilts.

lavender & alchemilla

This is the most restful of all garden-flower combinations, a subtle haze of color that stays beautifully understated. The pale green froth of alchemilla (or lady's mantle), one of those ambiguous plants whose blooms seem to be part of the foliage rather than separate flowerheads, is always cool and refreshing against all the harsher brights of a summer border. Its traditional pairing with lavender — alternate clumps of color spilling onto either side of a garden path or lawn — is inspired. Their gentle natures make them two of the easiest shades to live with, and, used together, they create an irresistible sense of quiet calm. Natural mixers with pale woods and mellow basketware, they themselves fade beautifully into soft grays and neutrals. As well as paints, fabrics, and ceramics, you will also find these shades in smoky-veined marble and lichen-covered stone. These materials can either be used as part of your furnishing plan or left in a garden setting where their muted tones will look even more at home.

Right: An old bleached-wood cabinet and peg rail emphasize the muted color scheme of green and mauve, creating the effect of a faded photograph in this country powder room.

Far right: Layers of soft green and lilac, seen one beyond another as you look through these doorways, contribute softly contrasting tones to a scheme of washed-out country house colors.

❍ To keep the effect muted, combine lilacs and greens with materials and colors that emphasize their natural character — stone, gray stripped wood, or the faded terra-cotta of old garden pots and bricks.

❍ For a fresher, more obviously floral feel, add plenty of white accents in woodwork and linens.

❍ These colors work almost everywhere, but are especially restful in bedrooms, living rooms, and floral-themed bathrooms.

❍ Try them as an alternative to the more commonly seen combination of pink and green — using lilac instead of pink gives a cooler, subtler effect.

rose & peony

We learn to be wary of mixing such heady colors as pinks and reds. The warmth and overwhelming richness of the combination are enough to deter most decorators — even without the risk that the result might be a little less sophisticated than we were hoping for.

The secret of working with these colors, however, is to have confidence. Trust in their natural toning contrasts to suggest harmonious shades that will sit comfortably together. With an even greater leap of faith, follow the lead of the vibrant colors that appear side by side in flowerbeds, florists' shops, and bouquets. You might falter if you stopped to think about what you were doing, but as long as you can envisage the glorious indulgence of velvety roses next to blowsy, full-petaled peonies, you won't lose heart.

Your furnishings don't need to be quite so rich, though. Take a single pale pink peony head and look for the deeper reds that bleed through it. All you need for a country dining room with a beautifully tranquil atmosphere is to use the palest shade as a background and pick out the stronger tones for fabrics, ceramics, and accessories, and use the very deepest tones, dark purply-browns, for furniture.

○ If the combination feels too strong, concentrate on the paler shades, adding plenty of white and a few darker accents to cool the scheme down.

○ The bolder colors will create a more contemporary effect, so back them up with clean, streamlined shapes and a few pieces of modern furniture.

○ Flashes of deep, bright pink — closer to fuchsia than rose — add drama and energy when combined with more sugary shades.

○ Remember that pinks and reds have a warming effect, so use them in rooms where you want to feel secure and enclosed.

Right: Traditional wainscoting adds contrasts and shadows to the pale pink paintwork, suggesting deeper tones that are then echoed in the chair fabric and in the dark wood furniture.

Far right: Pink walls and woodwork create a rich, warm setting with a strong sense of drama. Accents of deep peony red keep the effect sharp rather than sugary.

lupin & foxglove

Standing tall in cottage borders, the pink and purple flower-clad spires of lupins and foxgloves add structure and elegance among plants with a looser, more rambling habit. They may be nominally "wild," but their height and restraint create a natural sense of order, and their colors have an intensity that can't be ignored. Dark pinks and purples, moody and deep against garden foliage and enjoying the drama they bring to shady, woodland places, are individually striking and even more effective when used in combination. Rich and jewel-like, these are colors that conjure up luxury in the simplest setting, and provide a perfect balance between warm and cool. Use them for lustered materials like velvets, silks, and iridescent metals and they will add instant opulence; try them in soft woolens and woven plaids, and the absorbent quality of the fabric will emphasize their more muted, shadowy tones.

In some ways these are perfect evening colors, which will be brought to life in a candlelit dining room or a romantic bedroom. But their mutable nature, making the flowers equally at home in a sunny border or leafy corner, means that their pretty, feminine shades are also soft enough for bathrooms and living rooms.

Left: Delicate pink china acquires a dramatic look when accessorized with silk ribbon and enameled silverware in a deeper, richer purple.

Right: Both pink and purple take on a muted shadowy tone when used for soft woolens, blankets, and plaids, with floral pink details adding a fresher, more traditional touch.

❍ The balance between the two colors is the secret here, so don't be tempted to go for a single shade unless you want a very different effect. The pink is warmer and fresher, while the purple provides a deeper, moodier quality.

❍ Like all flower colors, the combination can be offset by small amounts of green to add some contrast and balance.

❍ This is probably too strong a combination to use for both walls and furnishings, but it works beautifully if you place pink and purple accents against a soft neutral background of cream or white to keep the colors looking fresh.

❍ Add plenty of white-painted woodwork so that the deeper, moodier tones of the colors don't become muddy or dominant.

❍ Keep the colors pale and discreet, with no dramatic contrasts or bold accents.

❍ Use soft pastel shades to reinvent simple wooden and metal furniture. Painting them with a coat of eggshell color will highlight interesting shapes and turn functional items into something much prettier.

❍ For cooler accents, introduce the occasional touch of ice blue. It isn't a color found among stocks or sweet peas, but it has the same quality of tone and adds a refreshing crispness.

❍ Stronger accents can only be included if they are transparent or translucent — such as the green glass lamp base shown at right. Dense colors will simply unbalance the scheme.

sweet peas & stocks

Pastels always mix more comfortably than other shades, and the beauty of a bed of sweet peas is the way random colors mingle together, their flimsy petals ruffled like tiny scraps of silk. There's sheer romance here, reminiscent of frilly party dresses, wedding cakes, and candied almonds. Pinks, mauves, creams, and whites, with their long, slender, pale green leaves and trademark twining stems, create an irresistible palette of gentle decorating color. Scented stocks contribute additional depth, with softly clustered blooms that look all the better for being mixed, several shades together, in vases and pitchers to make indoor displays. Use these delicate colors for paintwork and furnishings and you fill the house with year-round summer. Soft enough to provide gentle backgrounds as well as pretty fabrics and accessories, they are a wonderful combination of sweetness and subtlety, creating color schemes that are simply impossible to dislike.

The secret of their success is the barely-there color. Think of the care with which you tint cake frosting — adding the merest drop of deep red cochineal to turn the sugar mixture pale pink — and apply the same caution to all these shades. Start with as near to a pure white setting as you can get, then build up the pastel tones layer by layer, keeping them almost translucently pale and never letting the idea of "color" run wild and risk unbalancing the scheme. There's no need for patterns — blocks of plain pastels set against one another have just enough contrast for variety, and these pure colors have a simplicity and elegance that will carry the design without effort. Bedrooms, living rooms, bathrooms, and children's rooms will acquire an instant sense of discreet charm.

Far left: Decorated and furnished in the palest shades of pink, mauve, and green, this little living room has the delicate grace of a summer wedding cake. Elegant furniture designs in decorative metalwork and gilded wood add the finishing touch.

Left: Soft pinks and greens are used for this hand-painted lampshade, and the simple painted table provides a background of natural leaf green.

jasmine & honeysuckle

Some flowers are better known for their scent than their color, but that doesn't make them any less generous in providing decorating inspiration. The creamy white blossom that smothers jasmine and honeysuckle at the height of summer has a subtlety that is more usable than many brighter blooms, and its delicate pink accents — seen in the jasmine buds before they open and tinting the edges of the honeysuckle petals — add a warmer, faintly rosy glow. Looking almost edible in their delicious richness, these are the shades where the Flowers & Blossom palette comes closest to the Kitchen Garden palette (see page 106), with the simplicity of a country dairy and the coolness of buttermilk. There's nowhere these colors won't work, as long as you take care not to drown out their quiet tones with bold furnishings. Their softness is their strength, and you will lose that calming quality if you try to add bold contrasts or dramatic flourishes.

Below: A display of pink and white china lines the shelves of this painted cabinet, creating a light, summery feel in a traditional living room.

Right: An assortment of pillows piled up in a country bedroom captures the delicate colors of jasmine and honeysuckle in a collection of different fabrics.

○ Layering whites and creams together creates more depth of tone and greater interest than using either shade individually.

○ Don't add color to the mixture, other than the naturally occurring accents of pink and occasional touches of soft green.

○ Avoid harsh contrasts such as dark wood, which looks jarring and breaks up the smoothness of this creamy scheme.

○ The colors are very soft and absorb light, so you could benefit from adding occasional reflective surfaces such as glazed cupboards, lusterware, or mother-of-pearl flatware.

○ Look for pretty, small-scale floral fabrics in twining patterns that reflect the way honeysuckle grows.

KITCHEN GARDEN

KITCHEN GARDEN

FULL OF OLD-FASHIONED CHARM and farmhouse nostalgia, the colors of the kitchen garden are good enough to eat. Not confined to fruits and vegetables, they also reflect the delicious coolness of the dairy and the pantry. Here you'll find the natural shades of strawberries and cream, Granny Smith apples and fresh chopped herbs echoed in traditional country furnishings like red and white linen, creamware pitchers, and green and cream tiles. More dramatic accent colors include the purple of plums, figs, and eggplants; and the gold of pumpkins, squash, zucchini flowers, and orange marmalade. This is a homey, simple palette celebrating old-fashioned traditions of domesticity. It has a functional feel that adapts well to different rooms, so there's no need to restrict the colors to kitchen furnishings. Surprisingly versatile, these colors can shift from soft and creamy to sharp and zesty, from cool and fresh to rich and buttery. Take inspiration from the glowing jars of homemade preserves lined up on the pantry shelf, with their gingham lids and their labels hand-written on creamy parchment; the jewel-bright beads trimming the edges of cheesecloth food covers; and the soft, silvery greens of fat bunches of fresh, home-grown herbs hung up to dry.

Right: Silver-green herbs, translucent layers of crisp onion, and smooth, mellow creamware conjure up the colors of a pantry in a country kitchen.

THE KITCHEN GARDEN PALETTE

These ten shades provide a basic palette for recreating the colors found in the farmhouse kitchen and its adjoining vegetable garden. Soft dairy creams and crisp, crunchy whites provide plenty of easy-to-mix neutrals, with stronger colors coming from bright summer fruits, mellow leafy greens, and occasional splashes of dark, dramatic eggplant or beet. Keep your scheme relatively limited so that the effect is fresh and simple, like the domestic setting that inspired it. Use this palette to help you plan your initial colors, then draw in other variations from the combinations shown on the following pages.

radish heart

Crisp, pure white—almost an absence of color that, as a contrast to all the creams and bright reds of this palette, provides essential highlights in a cool neutral. Use it in layers with vanilla and buttermilk to offset their warmer tones, to keep the greens clean and fresh if they risk appearing murky, and to create fresh, simple schemes with bright tomato or raspberry.

vanilla

A very pale, slightly pink-tinged shade of cream perfect for creating softer highlights than pure white, but with enough depth of its own to act as a mellow background color or a gentle contrast to deeper tones. A traditional dairy shade, it mixes naturally with raspberry pinks and pea greens and can be layered with other creams and whites for a subtle combination.

buttermilk

The richest of the creams, with much more yellow in it. It can become rather sickly if used on its own, so add plenty of cooler, whiter accents, or use it in combination with the pinks and greens of the palette. For extra interest, look for fabrics that provide the color in a natural form and with plenty of texture, such as unbleached muslin, loose-woven butter muslin, and crinkly cheesecloth.

zucchini flower

The golden yellow of the trumpet-shaped zucchini flower. It contrasts beautifully with the fresh leaf greens and darker vegetation of the kitchen garden. Also the color of pumpkins and squashes and of jewel-bright marmalades lined up on pantry shelves, it adds a warmer, more luxurious note than the pale creams, and echoes the harvest shades of the Field & Woodland palette (page 18).

sage

A delicate, silvery green with a hint of blue in it, making it much cooler than the rest of the palette. Subtle and versatile, sage is a restful background color, soft and refreshing in bathrooms, bedrooms, and living rooms, and the sort of shade you can live with almost anywhere. It has a closer affinity with the Sun, Sea & Sky palette (page 48) than with most other leaf greens.

lettuce

A bright leaf green, crisp and full of energy, yet cool and refreshing—somehow managing to stimulate and to calm the spirit at the same time. If it feels too strong to use as a background color, try it for pillows and curtains (it's a delightful shade for summer cottons and linens), and mix it with floral pinks and blues as a change from the Kitchen Garden palette.

tomato

A bright, cheerful red, typical of kitchen linens and country ginghams. Useful for practical kitchens and playrooms and for creating settings with Scandinavian or American folk-style simplicity. Mix it with crisp radish-heart whites to cool down the warm color, and add touches of pink-tinged raspberry for a softer, prettier effect.

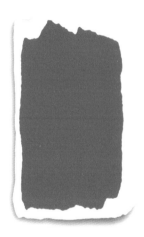

raspberry

A deep berry pink, deliciously pretty and full of summer flavor. It has plenty of subtlety, which makes it surprisingly usable. Best shown off by pale creams and yellows, it also mixes well with the gentle greens of the palette. Add plenty of textural variety—crushed velvets, shimmery silks, and soft woolens—to reflect the contrasts within the fruit itself.

cabbage

A deep, old-fashioned green, traditionally mixed with creams and whites, and also sympathetic to browns and russets. It has a muted, comfortable feel that works well in studies and libraries, along with old leather furniture, worn tapestries, antique needlepoint fabrics, and faded velvets. Use it to add an instant air of antiquity, and to maintain a solid, welcoming atmosphere throughout living areas.

eggplant

The surprise element in the palette—a deep, moody purple that adds unexpected drama but mixes well with creams, greens and golds. Use it sparingly, so that it has real impact where it appears, but enjoy the sense of luxury and indulge in touches of gilt or gold alongside it, to bring out its opulent character.

Far left: The deep red of redcurrants and raspberries for the curtains and seat cushions creates splashes of bright color against a buttermilk background. These shades are so potent that sparing use is all that's needed.

Center left: The bright cherry color of these traditional kitchen linens and the old-fashioned enamelware is softened by walls and furniture in vanilla so the overall effect is a gentle tone of pink rather than red.

Left: Dark plum is lightened by brighter touches of raspberry pink in this country kitchen, where the simple pine furniture and neat checked floor create an old-fashioned atmosphere.

Above: A bowl of tulips beautifully combines the colors of raspberries and cream against a vanilla background.

109

Left: These earthenware pitchers have the chunky practicality of a traditional farmhouse dairy, and the plain glaze in shades of buttermilk and heavy cream reinforces the simple, casual style of the table setting.

Below: Pale sage cabinets and cream walls provide a mellow setting for this homey kitchen. Traditional linens patterned with bands of cherry red and dark cabbage green add stronger color against the plain stripped furniture.

Right: The mixed greens of herbs and spices create a subtle palette of decorating inspiration. Here, the pale green of fennel seeds is tinged with a golden glow against the pure white of the porcelain pestle and mortar.

Far right: Soft, creamy paint shades work as comfortably in bathrooms as in kitchens, especially in combination with traditional wainscoting and neat, scrubbed floorboards.

Below right: The gentle combination of green and cream, reminiscent of the dark leaves surrounding a head of crisp cauliflower, can be freshened with highlights of pure white and even gilded for a more luxurious effect.

Below far right: The herb garden is a source of softer, subtler greens. Silvery sage works well for painted furniture, its pale color cool and light-reflective. To create a leaf design, use a laurel or bayleaf stencil and brush with a lighter shade of cream or mint green.

Left: Cream enamel and green-glazed china combine the fresh, summery feel of the kitchen garden with the mellow colors of the traditional pantry. Blue and white may be the classic choice for tableware, but green and cream have their own nostalgic charm.

Below: A faded country-house living room decorated in deliciously edible shades of raspberries and cream, with hints of plum and gooseberry adding deeper accents.

Right: The pantry supplies its own palette of whites and creams, perfect for layering one on top of another in subtle decorating schemes.

Far right: The creamy yellow curtains and covers of this tranquil bedroom are flecked with touches of raspberry pink and deeper flashes of bold color.

radish heart & tomato

○ Use paint to revamp old furniture for a neat red and white scheme, and paint floorboards white to provide a clean, fresh background.

○ Keep the emphasis on white rather than red, using touches of bold color to add contrast and definition.

○ Look for simple fabrics that reflect the practicality of the colors — ginghams, stripes, and small floral sprigs are ideal.

Kitchen garden colors tend to fall into two distinct categories — the mellow wholesomeness of creams and greens and the crisper, crunchier shades, which are energetic, invigorating, and generally more refreshing. Red and white ginghams or striped linen dish towels, bright painted furniture, and cheerful appliances in primary colors all reflect a no-nonsense mood that cuts through the gentle, earthy tones of traditional country furnishings.

Slice into a bunch of fresh garden radishes, and the contrast of crisp white center against the crimson outer skin is startling. Add the brighter, orangey red of tomato, and the result is slightly warmer, but still very bold. This is a sharp, uncompromising mix, its strength coming from its simplicity. You can't dilute the scheme with pastels,

neutrals, or half-shades — these colors demand to be used as they are — but despite their briskness, they are surprisingly versatile. As well as being perfect for country kitchens and bathrooms, their down-to-earth quality can create neat, uncluttered living rooms and bright, cheerful bedrooms.

The beauty of working with such uncomplicated colors is that they allow you a little more freedom in adding accessories. Where prettier shades run the risk of becoming frilly and overblown, the simplicity of a red and white scheme won't be undermined by the occasional decorative lampshade or floral-sprigged pillowcase. Lace, braid, and eyelet add softer touches without looking fussy, and country-style details are perfectly at home in a red and white kitchen.

Left: Crisp white towels trimmed with red rickrack add a neat touch in bathrooms. White linens are smart and traditional and provide a fresher look than mixed colors do.

Right: A checked cupboard lining matches the linen-bound notebooks and picks up the colors of the red and white china on this dresser.

Right: Mismatched chairs and flea-market finds can be freshened up with a quick coat of paint to suit your kitchen color scheme. Bright red gadgets and enamel storage containers add a practical, cheerful feel, while plain white tableware has an everyday simplicity that always looks right.

rosemary & sage

The colors of the herb garden are so distinctive that you can almost smell them. Gentle and soporific or fresh and tangy, they each have their own character and the subtlety to work in almost any country setting. Among the most usable shades are soft, silvery sage, with its velvet leaves and mellow fragrance, and the steely blue-green of the rosemary bush. Naturally calming, they mix beautifully with grays, mauves, and all kinds of blues — from the unexpected bright blooms of borage and sweet rocket to the haze of flowers that hovers above a patch of lavender. Slate floors and counters, the dull sheen of pewter, the cool glow of chrome and aluminum kitchen appliances — they all bring out the best in pale herb greens. Combine them with warm cream tiles or bright white paintwork, and see how these subtle colors create a restrained, elegant background wherever you use them. Entry halls, living rooms, kitchens, and studies all respond beautifully to their quiet, light-reflective quality. If you want to add stronger accents, look for furniture in dark, purply-brown wood, which provides plenty of contrast while maintaining the cool tone of the overall scheme.

Left: A little painted table holds a jug of mixed greenery and smoky-blue flowers, providing accents of slightly darker green against the pale apple-colored wall.

Right: A tranquil kitchen in the softest of sage greens, with touches of light blue paintwork on the paneling above the counters. Even the sleek modern appliances can't undermine the mellow, old-fashioned feel of this gentle color scheme.

○ Maintain the pale, almost neutral color scheme by avoiding bright colors — restrict accent shades to the natural blues and purples of herb flowers.

○ Add plenty of cool neutrals — marble counters and washstands, stoneware containers, and white china.

○ Use the combination in rooms that adjoin the yard, so that you bring outdoor colors into the house and reflect the shades of trees and foliage.

○ Use it to open up small rooms. The pale colors are light-reflective and space-making, and are softer than bright white.

raspberries & cream

○ Indulge in the romance of these easy, restful colors. Even people who wouldn't normally use pink will find them amazingly usable.

○ Start by concentrating on the cream element of the color scheme, adding sparing amounts of raspberry to see what effect it creates. Once you can gauge the balance, you'll be able to introduce more color confidently.

○ Experiment with different strengths of color, from the palest pastel tints to deeper, juicier shades that add more drama.

○ Be prepared to vary the shade of the cream you use — some yellowy creams may start to look rather sickly, whereas cool vanilla will have a lighter, fresher effect.

The most delicious of combinations, this romantic, summery mixture is also one of the easiest to use. It is the kind of color scheme that works in kitchens and bathrooms as effectively as in bedrooms and living rooms; that suits bright, south-facing rooms as well as gloomier settings; and that can be warm and comforting as well as cool and refreshing. Raspberry is a surprisingly subtle shade, its deeper tones rich and glowing like the center of the fruit itself, but also with a paler, softer quality, reflecting that velvety surface and fragile, crumbling texture. The addition of cream can either highlight the brightness of the pink, making it seem even fresher and crisper by contrast, or dilute it into a gentler blend, like juice and cream swirled together to create a pretty pastel. You have the choice of using these different shades individually to give the room a specific style or combining them in mixed layers to provide a more complex color scheme.

Below: Pink and white checks on an armchair create a pretty, inviting setting and provide gentle color in this sun-filled living room.

Right: Deep raspberry pinks are layered with paler pastel bedcovers against cream-painted walls. The enamel jug on the windowsill shows the raspberry and cream colors swirled together on a single surface.

❍ Mix different shades of green together, drawing inspiration from the colors and textures of the kitchen garden.

❍ Use the darker colors to create calm and quiet in studies, or atmosphere and drama in formal dining rooms. The brighter, lighter shades will be refreshing in bathrooms, kitchens, and bedrooms.

❍ To vary the palette, add accents of lively yellows, cool blues and lilacs, or striking raspberry pinks.

peapod & asparagus

Stronger, brighter greens can feel daunting to work with until you accept that their natural quality makes them uniquely suited to creating comfortable rooms with timeless elegance. Where other colors can jar or pall or look as though they had tried just a little too hard to create the right effect, green has a simple, organic quality and a refreshing, rejuvenating character that you won't easily tire of. Kitchen garden produce is a surprising source of color inspiration because it contains so many shades within its shoots and leaves. Look at the way the green of a leek or a scallion fades from dark to bright, then to pale, and finally to white, providing a complete harmonizing color palette as effectively as any paint chart. Now split open a fava-bean shell and see the crisp contrast between the bright shell, the soft white of the lining, and the row of pale beans nestling in it. Picture the combination as white woodwork against emerald-painted walls, or a glossy checked backsplash of green and white ceramic tiles, and see how fresh and clean the colors are. They are perfect for kitchens and bathrooms, and intriguing for the first impression they create in an entry hall. Their invigorating spirit can also be put to good use in studies and libraries and, indeed, wherever you want to encourage concentration and harness energy. Because different greens appear in a naturally random mixture in the herb garden and vegetable patch, they seem to have a natural place alongside one another in interior designs, too — and that comfortable partnership makes them easier to use as decorating colors than you might expect. Enjoy their sense of refreshing calm, and have fun experimenting with this unusual palette.

Left: Deep green walls and cool white woodwork create a quiet, calm workspace in this comfortable study. Flashes of brighter leaf and apple greens add a livelier, stimulating feel.

Above right: Bright green walls, as fresh as crisp peapods, glow in the sunlight of this entry hall window. Garden flowers reflect the color in its purest form, highlighting the individual blues and yellows that combine to form the various shades of green.

Right: Handmade ceramic tiles, their uneven surfaces catching the light and dappling the color, are fresh and summery in green and white.

eggplant & zucchini flower

Be careful when choosing eggplant colors — avoid the hotter, crimson shades and stick to cool, smoky purples.

If you want a cooler, more restrained effect, add details in silver or pewter rather than gold, and plenty of plain white paint and ceramics.

Don't try to add too much eggplant at once. This is a very potent color and you need only a small quantity to produce a dramatic result.

Deep and dramatic, eggplant is one of those colors that can take on a life of its own once you let it loose in your home. Generally too overpowering for those with nervous dispositions, and too bold to be used with safety if you're at all worried about what other people think, it has a strong, moody character that needs handling with care and restraint. Have faith in its richness, though, and you'll find it a fabulous source of luxury, capable of giving any room a distinctive air. It's particularly good for bedrooms and bathrooms — places where you want to indulge your senses and where you can cope with color schemes that you probably wouldn't want to live with 24 hours a day. Use it for satin bedcovers, crystal lamp droplets, lusterware, and occasional areas of paintwork. You needn't go for excessive opulence — combining it with plain painted surfaces, natural wood, simple basketware, and mellow, well-used furniture will balance the drama of the color and make the whole room feel comfortable as well as luxurious.

Don't let the deep purple tones become gloomy or oppressive: the bright gold of pumpkins, squashes, fresh zucchini flowers, and marmalade makes a perfect companion to eggplant, emphasizing its natural richness but at the same time providing sunnier highlights. Yellowy-orange paint colors and fabrics can both be used to good effect, while gold leaf and gilded details will add even more drama. Look for gilt mirror and picture frames, or rub old wooden frames with touches of gilt cream, and use old brass door handles rather than sleek new chrome or steel. Your aim should be to keep the color scheme romantic, and perhaps just a touch exotic. If the gold feels too bright, add touches of soft green, too — the color of the eggplant stalk and zucchini leaves. Green works beautifully with purple and creates a quieter, more natural effect.

Right: The dark purple exterior of this bath tub gives the whole room a sense of luxury, even though the dramatic color is offset by simple accessories and plain painted floorboards.

Below: Ripe figs capture the subtle moodiness of the color scheme, as the green skin of the young fruit gives way to mature purple.

kale & cauliflower

A love-it-or-hate-it color, green hasn't always been the most popular of decorating shades. But there's a restful, comforting feel about its old-fashioned character, making it useful for kitchens and bathrooms, and the natural leaf shades of the kitchen garden translate very effectively into furnishing and paint colors. To see how these colors work together, look at the way individual fruits and vegetables combine harmonious shades in a single surface, as in the light veining that runs through the brighter green of kale or cabbage, or the pale creaminess of cauliflower florets against the darker leaves surrounding them.

Left: Deep green paint defines this bedroom's shape and architectural detail, creating a harmonious contrast with the pale green walls.

Below: The old-fashioned colors are perfectly suited to classic porcelain, especially with gilt decoration.

○ There's a slight risk of greens looking institutional. To avoid associating the color with schools or hospitals, add touches of crisp white to freshen the scheme, or rich gold to lend a sense of luxury.

○ Take advantage of the schoolroom feel and use its practical, industrious character to provide a good working environment in your study or office.

○ Use it in old-fashioned kitchens to conjure up a dairy feel, adding plenty of chunky cream china, simple enamel, and practical wooden accessories.

○ Pick up the richer creams for a more indulgent effect in living rooms and dining rooms, and add touches of gold to make it feel more elegant.

greengage & buttermilk

○ Occasional touches of other clean, fresh berry colors — such as red-checked kitchen linens — add brighter accents.

○ Darker greens added sparingly will help to "anchor" the scheme with more definition if the pale green color is looking too thin and acidic.

○ For more dramatic accents, try touches of deep purply blues and reds. Greengages are close in tone to white grapes, so envisage the combination of purple and white grapes together and aim for a similar contrast.

○ Pick up on the natural, leafy quality of the color and mix it with other earth tones, or try shades from the Field & Woodland palette (see page 18).

Greengage plums are an unexpected delight. Whereas the pinks and reds of summer berries instantly suggest sweetness and romance, the pale yellow-green skin of the greengage is less immediately appealing until you strip away its peel to reveal the glorious golden flesh beneath. What brings it to life, both as a flavor and as a color, is the addition of cream, which enriches its texture and softens its acid tones into something deliciously subtle and tangy. This light, almost luminous shade has a soft greeny-gold glow that blends gently into muted, neutral country settings, contributing a hint of understated color without trying to dominate the whole scheme. The color combination is especially good in kitchens, where the natural creaminess mixes well with old-fashioned fittings and scrubbed paintwork, and in studies and libraries, where its understated color suits the quiet setting and contrasts gently with the worn leather of old books and furniture. Experiment with it in sunrooms, too, where the dappled sunlight that filters through the trees outside will pick up the yellow tones and add sparkling highlights. And use it for rubbed or distressed paintwork, layering shades of green and yellow together so that the broken finish reflects the translucent color of the fruit.

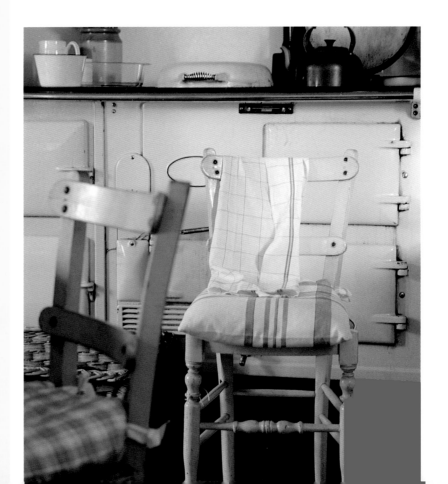

Left: The yellowy-green paintwork of the kitchen chairs stands out against the softer, creamier color of the range. The shift in tone is very subtle, but the chairs have a sharper, cleaner note.

Right: The faded, streaky green of the bookcase suits the comfortably studious air of the room, with mellow cream walls and just a touch of stronger, deeper color in the paintwork of the distant door.

strawberry, apple & mint

○ Keep the greens fresh and pale: too strong a color may be hard to live with and will create a very harsh contrast with the red.

○ Avoid having too much natural wood that might dull the colors and lead to a "muddy" mixture. Go for painted woodwork that will freshen and lighten the scheme.

○ Keep the furniture light and graceful, opting for carved wood and wrought-iron designs rather than chunkier pieces whose solid shape could make the color scheme feel heavy or overpowering.

This is a scheme that is redolent of summer. Creamy white, like a sliced apple, the mixed greens of apple skins and mint leaves, and the fresh red of cut strawberries provide the perfect blend of crisp, cool colors. The contrasting shades balance each other beautifully, so that no single one predominates, with the cooler greens offsetting the splashes of bright red, and clean whites preventing the green from appearing too muted or gray. Strong greens and reds can fight if used too liberally together, but if you stick to pale mint, sage, or mossy tones, and mix them with pink-tinged berry reds, the combination will stay crisp, fresh, and easy to live with. You may be able to find a fabric or wallpaper that incorporates both colors on a cream or white background — floral patterns provide the right color mixture if you can't find fruit designs. Otherwise, try experimenting with contrasting paintwork, either using details in one color to add accents to a larger area of the other, or picking out details in red and green in a predominantly neutral room.

Left: Fresh white paintwork offsets the pale mint green walls, while accents of bright strawberry red highlight the bedcover and ceiling beams in this summery bedroom.

Right: A delicate pink and green scalloped border, hung with tiny fabric beads, trims this cream linen lampshade and adds a pretty, Victorian-style finish to the green-painted base.

SLATE & STONE

SLATE & STONE

THE MOST ELEGANT OF COUNTRY COLORS, these nearly neutral shades work as a muted version of stronger schemes. Blues and mauves fade into gentle gray; pinks and yellows bleach into soft beige or sand. The effect is like an old photo, mellow and timeless, with an organic quality that feels very natural and provides a perfect backdrop for country life. The cool grays of slate and charcoal, the warmer tones of clay, terra-cotta, and sandstone, and the pretty shades provided by delicately veined marble all provide subtle inspiration for furnishing colors, as well as supplying actual materials for you to incorporate in your home. Texture becomes increasingly

Right: A stone-colored linen napkin, trimmed at the edges with rough-textured shells to weight the fabric, creates a practical food cover for a country kitchen.

important if you are working with predominantly neutral shades, so this chapter includes ideas for different surfaces that will accent contrasts and create interesting depth and shadow. Make the most of natural, textured fabrics such as linen, burlap, and corduroy, renovate traditional slate and flagstone floors, and enjoy the variegated, uneven tone of timeless wall finishes such as raw plaster and exposed brickwork. Plain white ceramics and pale, creamy terra-cotta shades provide gentle highlights against the darker, muddier shades. Accessories can be kept to a minimum — the beauty of this look is its simplicity.

THE SLATE & STONE PALETTE

These ten shades provide a neutral palette that recreates the colors of the countryside's natural materials. The subtle tones are wonderfully satisfying to use because they let you build up layers of character and contrast without swamping the room with any definite sense of color. Look for a good balance of warm and cool shades, and keep the different whites handy to add gentle highlights so that the scheme doesn't become muddy. Use this palette to plan your basic colors, then create your own subtle effects by drawing in variations from the combinations shown on the following pages.

alabaster

A pale porcelain white, which is clean, light-reflective, and almost translucent. It creates an elegant background color for graceful, decorative furnishings, and adds delicate highlights if used for woodwork and details. Fine china and white enamel can supply it in the form of tableware, and crisp linen provides softer lines. Layer it with warmer whites and creams for a richer effect.

limestone

A warmer, more textured white, comfortable as a background shade and easy to supply with paintwork, fabric, furniture, and ceramics. This is the kind of color that works comfortably on uneven surfaces and paneled walls, where its mellow tone gives a simple, rustic feel. It makes a good contrast with wooden beams and floorboards and with other natural materials.

sandstone

A soft, pale yellow, beautifully warm but with a hint of cool gray that tones down any tendency to brightness. It provides a stronger sense of color when used against completely neutral shades, but is still subtle enough to keep the overall effect restrained and understated. Sandstone works particularly well in combination with balancing grays and natural slate blues.

marble

The palest of grays, a silvery shade that's barely more than white darkened by shadow, but that can also provide sparkling highlights of its own. A good alternative to white for woodwork and painted furniture, it can be found in soft, matte fabrics such as wool and felt, and in the delicate shimmer of silks, velvets, and sheer voiles. Use it to cool down an over-bright white room.

putty

Muted and mutable, a subtle gray-brown shade that seems able to adapt to surrounding colors and surfaces with little effort. It sometimes seems to have a pinkish-chocolatey bloom; at other times it can appear as a cooler gray. An easy background color to live with, it's also very versatile for woodwork and can be readily found in neutral fabrics such as corduroy, linen, and burlap.

clay

A warm, rustic color that provides a range of shades perfect for country furnishings. Rich and earthy, it is best suited to simple fabrics such as woolens and corduroys, but it can take on a more luxurious look in velvets and chenilles. It also supplies effective texture in hand-thrown ceramics and unfinished wood surfaces, giving country rooms a robust, practical feel.

terra-cotta

Similar to clay, but usually veering slightly toward the redder tones. Like clay, it can conjure up a range of shades and effects, but the overall feel is hotter and drier, sometimes giving a powdery look. Almost a deeper version of plaster pink, it is tremendously comfortable, has subtle depth, and is good for recreating sun-bleached, Mediterranean styles.

granite

An imposing shade, dark and solid, but warmer than the undiluted gray tones because it incorporates an element of reddish brown. It provides a rich sense of drama and atmosphere and works well in sophisticated, tailored rooms with a more contemporary feel. Don't overdo it, or the strong color will feel oppressive; use small quantities with grays and whites.

slate

A mid-gray with plenty of character. Far more definite than marble, slate is good for supplying strength and atmosphere, especially when set against softer, paler colors. It becomes calm and restful if used to balance warm reds and yellows. Make the most of its austere, down-to-earth quality by combining it with Shaker-style furnishings and simple, understated room designs.

charcoal

The drama queen of the Slate & Stone palette — a deep, moody tone with a hint of purple. Dark and leaden, it creates wonderful shadows and striking focal points, yet its inky, blue-black nature also works beautifully in intricate monochrome patterning on fabrics and wallpapers. Cool and classic, it's the color to call on when you want to make an effortless impact.

Above: The old brickwork and weathered wood of this doorway have faded to the same soft, muted shade, creating a warm, sunlit entrance to the cottage. Somewhere between gray and brown, it has a gentle honeyed appearance.

Right: A bleached gray cabinet is filled with ocher-colored ceramics, combining warm and cold neutrals together against the rich, polished floorboards.

Far right: Moody grays and browns create a formal, dramatic living room with classical touches — an elegantly curved pitcher on a table and a bust on the windowsill contrast with the simpler plaid pillows and painted wood.

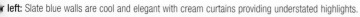

r left: Slate blue walls are cool and elegant with cream curtains providing understated highlights.

ft: Pale gray paintwork gives this side table and cabinet a Scandinavian-style finish, with plain wood
nters and handles maintaining the simple farmhouse look and adding warmer tones.

ove: Painting the interior of the cupboard a warm chocolate brown to contrast with the slate blue doors
ates an earthy Shaker-style effect. Plain and patterned stoneware adds monochrome detailing.

ht: The checked chair cover provides a single flash of color against neutral creams and grays.

Far left: Deep sepia tones are light and elegant when used in delicate toile de Jouy patterns, adding just a touch of drama against a cool white and cream background. Plain white linens and ceramics create the simplest of table settings, with cream-painted woodwork giving the color scheme a little more depth and richness.

Left: The faintest pink blush lifts these almost-white flowers out of the neutral background of the windowsill.

Below left: Muted stone colors acquire more character when painted onto wood paneling; the shadows create areas of light and dark, giving the surface accent and definition. Fabrics in different textures add more depth and interest.

Below right: Different shades of white add their own highlights against the pale gray walls of this tranquil bedroom. The painted furniture contributes a layer of deeper tone; the only pure color is the pink fabric of the lampshade.

○ Think of slate and sandstone as diluted versions of blue and yellow and use them to create subtler effects — contented rather than happy, restful rather than refreshing.

○ Adjust the balance between the two colors according to whether you want to cool down or warm up the setting. Extra sandstone will be brighter and sunnier; extra slate will tone down strong sunlight.

○ Look for natural materials that repeat the colors. Pewter and gunmetal accessories supply additional grays, while wood, basketware, and exposed brickwork emphasize the soft sandstone shades.

○ Introduce occasional highlights of pure white china or linen for a fresher, brighter effect.

slate & sandstone

Left: Pale sandstone walls and a wood-plank floor create a mellow background for slate-gray kitchen cabinets.

Below: Here, the two shades combine for a rustic effect.

Below right: Gray gingham fabric and a striped throw echo the cool-colored woodwork in this pretty yellow sitting room, softening the glare of the sun.

The beauty of neutral schemes is the way that warm and cool tones balance each other naturally without the need for obvious color. Shadowy slate gray and the soft creamy ocher of sandstone are a perfect mix because of this balance — wonderfully mellow, but with enough variety and contrast to create essential depth and atmospheric shadows. Look at the gray tones that appear on a sandy-yellow wall when the light leaves it, and you can see how comfortably the two shades enhance one another, the darker color drawing out the natural character of the lighter one. The same is true of gray surfaces where sunlight touches them, gilding their somber mood with a layer of warmth.

The rich glow of a wooden countertop against a slate-gray cabinet is enough to conjure up the effect. A slab of slate set on top of an ocher-painted cupboard behaves in a similar way. Strengthened into blue and gold, these colors would have the invigorating freshness of the Sun, Sea & Sky palette, but diluted into this muted form, they become gentle and restful — shades that you can live with every day. They provide a practical backdrop to kitchens and well-traveled hallways, and are pretty enough to create elegant living and dining rooms. Use them as an alternative to brighter blues and yellows, and try them if you want a neutral effect without losing all sense of color.

putty & limestone

The subtlest neutrals manage to convey a sense of texture along with their color. The bleached, chalky look of limestone white — soft and powdery, sometimes with a green tinge reminiscent of moss, lichen, and natural weathering — produces this effect. The chocolatey gray-browns of putty shades are similarly expressive, pale and velvety like moleskin, with hints of silvery pink that catch the light beautifully. Use these colors in combination with elegantly carved furniture and delicate crystal accessories, and you create a cool, restrained setting in which the muted neutrals are highlighted by a frosting of white accents. The simplicity of the palette lends itself to textured plain linen fabrics,

rough burlaps, and understated Shaker-style checks, but its pale delicacy is also perfect for prettier, daintier fabrics like coffee-colored lace, beaded oyster silks, and crisp, white eyelet. Echo the tracery of lace with intricate, filigree wallpaper designs, and with jacquard or damask fabric weaves in which a pale pattern lifts itself out of a tonal background. Hang panels of embroidered voile at the window to increase this subtle tone-on-tone effect. The key to this combination is its softness, so you need to keep the finish mellow. Stick to pale white or cream walls and woodwork, with painted or pickled-wood furniture and stripped wood floors or natural matting.

○ This combination produces a different effect depending on the accents you add — use cream for a gentle, mellow contrast or white for a fresher look.

○ Use these sophisticated colors to add elegance to a small room, keeping the background mostly pure white or cream, with putty-colored accents insuring that the effect is restrained and down to earth.

○ Add plenty of texture to enrich the mix and give the simple colors a sense of warmth and comfort.

○ Avoid darker woods, which create too strong a contrast.

Left: Painted furniture and simple check fabrics provide mellow putty tones against the limestone white background. A table set with crystal and white china adds sparkling highlights.

Right: A delicate tracery of white highlights the coffee-colored wallpaper, with white wainscoting and paintwork adding their own details and shadows. Layered covers in creams, whites, and putty shades are piled on the elegant carved bed.

plaster & terra-cotta

If you are looking for warmth and richness among your neutrals, you need materials that provide plenty of variety within their basic shades. Raw plaster is one of the most subtle, a mellow mushroom pink that changes shade as it dries, creating a stippled surface full of inspiring tones. Terra-cotta is even more versatile, with tiles ranging from pale biscuit cream through pinks and oranges to deep burgundy-browns, depending on the color of the original clay. Use these ready-made palettes to pick shades that harmonize naturally, either keeping to a narrow range of plaster pinks and beiges for an earthy, unfinished look, or incorporating stronger contrasts of cream and orange for more drama. Look for tweed and plaid fabrics that weave the colors into a gentle mixture, or use mottled terra-cotta for a tiled floor or wall that combines different depths of tone in a single surface. Details in cream or gold enrich the effect even more. If the look is too warm for comfort, cool it down with slate blues and grays or cool metals such as chrome and steel.

○ **New plaster always needs to dry completely before it can be painted or papered over, so you have plenty of time to decide if you like the raw effect and to draw inspiration from its changing shades.**

○ **Remember that the color of terra-cotta changes as it weathers or if you seal it.**

Far left: A plain wooden counter and mosaic-effect terra-cotta tiles are rich and earthy against walls the color of raw plaster.

Left: Slate gray pillows add a cooler, darker tone to pale walls stippled in soft mushroom pink.

Right: A woolen throw in pink and gray checks casts a layer of comfortable warmth over this armchair.

○ **Look for fabrics and soft textures in these two shades so that the colors aren't confined to the hard surfaces.**

charcoal & granite

○ Use metal furniture and finishes to provide elements of charcoal color — pewter lamp bases and tableware, black-leaded fire grates, and wrought-iron furniture and curtain poles.

○ Make the most of natural wood to give the color scheme structure. Ceiling beams, solid, rustic furniture, and heavy plank doors all add definition.

○ Look for materials that supply natural rich browns and dark reds, such as leather furniture and the darker shades of terra-cotta floor tiles.

○ Keep the background light and plain, and add the darker colors in details so that they don't seem overpowering or gloomy.

○ This is a strong color combination, so stick to plain surfaces and simple patterns to keep the effect understated and elegant.

Stone colors lose their "neutral" identity tag once you move into the deeper, darker shades. Somber grays and browns, their intense tones creating instant focal points, are never going to fade into the background or be taken for granted. Introducing them to a room promises drama and atmosphere, for these colors have a sense of character that demands to be taken seriously. Dark charcoal gray is particularly versatile, with a cool, purply quality that sets moody shadows against lighter shades. Try it in contrasting materials, mixing shiny satins with soft, matte woolens so that you recreate the way the light plays on the different surfaces of charcoal — glinting on its smooth, sheared planes and being absorbed by the rougher sides. The severity of the color is reminiscent of starchy Victorian restraint and old-fashioned tailoring, but it also has a cool simplicity that adapts beautifully to contemporary style and plain, understated furnishings. Combine it with rough-textured wood and pale, chalky paint shades and it acquires an almost unbeatable natural elegance, calm and sophisticated in living rooms and dining rooms, and quiet enough to use in bedrooms, too.

Granite supplies an additional quality of tone, its rugged solidity tempered by the mottled, flecked surface found in kitchen sinks and counters. Sometimes gray but often a dark brown or a pinkish red, it mixes comfortably with charcoal shades, accentuating their deeper tones and providing a warmer, more textured feel that enriches the whole effect.

Left: Warm brown bedcovers add granite-flecked color, with gray-green paintwork and gray-painted metal tables sounding a cooler note.

Right: Deep gray covers and pillows and the rich brown of the curtain provide a dramatic contrast with the white bedlinen and pale paneled wall, creating a somber, sophisticated bedroom setting.

marble & flint

Two of the prettiest forms of stone combine here for a color scheme of subtle variety and gentle contrasts. The beauty of these materials is the way they incorporate both warm and cool tones within their intriguing surfaces — the veining in a slab of marble can drift from gray to pink, and a flint wall may well contain blues, corals, and honey golds as well as the more expected blacks and grays. Take inspiration from these ready-made mixes, confident that the same shades will work comfortably together and that the neutral color schemes they create will be full of interest and sparkle. Gray used on its own runs the risk of appearing cold and gloomy, but if you add touches of warmer pink or gold, the mood is instantly lifted. Honey-colored wooden floorboards or furniture will lighten a gray-painted room, and pretty pastel fabrics will offset the severity of a gray marble fireplace. For more inspiration, take a look at the colors explored in the Sun, Sea & Sky chapter (pages 44–71), and introduce some of the shades found among shells and pebbles to provide subtly warm accents.

❍ Look at the way colors are combined in slabs of natural marble and use these as guidelines for combining colors.

❍ Degrees of warmth and cool are relative, so contrast different shades to see how they react. A soft blue looks warmer and prettier when set against a moody gray.

Far left: Pale blue walls and a gray and white painted floor give this landing a flint-cool air, but stripped wood furniture and gilded picture frames add warmer tones.

Left: This little living room emphasizes the pretty pinks and blues found in flint and marble, creating soft highlights against the austere gray wall.

Right: Honey-gold floorboards and coral-colored shells contrast with the cool pale gray of the painted chair.

clay & limestone

Sometimes you want a richer mix than most neutrals are able to supply, which is where clay tones come in handy. Offering the same variety and versatility as terra-cotta, clay has the fuller, riper quality of the raw material, rather than the drier, crisper finish of the fired terra-cotta colors. From pale porcelain creams to rich dark browns, it can also throw up red-golds and muddy grays, depending on the consistency of the earth it's made from and the metals it contains. This robust palette lets you create stronger, more dramatic color schemes, setting light shades beside dark ones in moody contrasts, and adding warmer mid-tones for comfort. Natural wood can provide many of these hues — pickled or bleached to create the paler tones, waxed or polished for greater depth. The chalky white of limestone adds brighter highlights in paintwork, linen, and ceramics. For extra energy you can include flashes of bright orange, which accentuate the richest clay accents and lift the whole effect out of the everyday and functional with a layer of more flamboyant color.

Left: The comfortable warmth of this country dining room is the result of a beautifully balanced color scheme, with rich clay tones providing a range of browns against the simple white-painted walls, chairs, and floorboards, and cushions adding flashes of bright gold.

Right: Limestone white walls and pale pickled floorboards create a cool background for darker, muddier browns and grays.

❍ Limestone white is one of the most versatile background shades, especially on uneven surfaces such as wood paneling and floorboards.

❍ Use the full extent of the clay palette to add rich depth of color with warm browns, golds, and reds.

❍ Use the brightest shades to add colorful accents to neutral color schemes, balancing the stark contrast of dark against light with cheerful mid-tones for a livelier look.

❍ Mix natural and painted woods for a comfortable, informal effect, rather than trying to make everything match.

○ Use these warm tones to enrich a cool, north-facing room, adding occasional touches of brighter white to keep the color scheme fresh.

○ Combine them with clean lines and simple furnishings, letting the warmth of the colors soften the austere setting with mellow, welcoming comfort.

○ Pick up their richer tones in luxurious fabrics such as silks and velvets, and add touches of gilding in fine china and picture frames to give a more elegant effect.

○ If the clay shades feel too rich and earthy, shift the balance to increase the paler, sandstone element, so that the overall feel is creamy yellow with a few stronger accents.

sandstone & clay

The buttery warmth of these colors almost belongs in the dairy shades of the Kitchen Garden palette, but they have an earthy, muddy quality that is more in keeping with natural stone and soil. Simple enough to use in the most rustic setting, but with a richness equally well suited to elegant country living rooms, this is a combination to conjure up mellow, comfortable charm wherever you need it. The key to its restfulness is the lack of any bright highlights or dramatic contrasts. Instead, use natural wood, rush-seated furniture, and woven coir matting on the floor to provide a background of muted warmth. Keep the paintwork to a narrow range of gentle honey shades so that the room acquires a single overall color tone.

Let fabrics and furniture provide their own natural shadows, such as the narrow stripe of old-fashioned blankets, the graining and paneling of woodwork, or the outline of a decorative chair back or an iron-framed bed against the plain color of the wall behind it. Look for fabrics that combine a subtle variety of shades in their patterns, such as muted stripes and plaids, or layer a plain silk or linen curtain with a lining in a deeper tone so that it provides contrast without becoming a distracting focal point. Gentle highlights can be added with parchment whites and warm creams, soft neutrals that add texture rather than light. And if the scheme becomes too rich for comfort, you can simply introduce a few elements of cool blues or metallic grays to tone down the warmth and restore the neutral balance.

Far left: Old-fashioned dormitory-style bed frames create stark outlines against the mellow sandstone wall. Traditional blankets and coir matting keep the effect warm but simple.

Left: The subtle stripes of the curtain pick up the different tones of the honey-colored room, including the pale wood of the corner cabinet, and the darker wood of the little chair in the foreground.

chalk & graphite

This is a combination of clean contrasts, the darker blue-gray tones of natural graphite creating deep shadows against cool white. The expanse of pale, chalky background keeps the overall effect light, with patches of black, navy blue, or dark gray adding accents and details. You may find these in fabrics patterns or paint colors, but they can also be supplied more subtly by natural materials such as metalwork or ebony, which create elegant patterns and silhouettes. The result is fresh and bright, although it may be too chilly for most north-facing rooms. The bright white may help to compensate for a lack of natural sunlight, but the effect will still be overwhelmingly cool. These understated colors have a close affinity with the nautical shades of the Sun, Sea & Sky palette (page 48), so if you want to add a little more color, you could introduce pinks and yellows to warm up the effect, or blues and greens to echo the natural grays and keep the room cool and fresh. Small touches are all that's necessary to enrich the mix and lift the combination out of its monochrome simplicity.

Left: Touches of gray-blue patterning on the fabric, a wooden picture frame, and decorative wrought-iron handles on the chest of drawers provide occasional darker accents against the chalk-white walls, furniture, and fabric.

Right: The dark stripes of the bed canopy and chair cover are crisp and stark against the white-painted furniture, floorboards, and foreground walls. The mid-gray of the far walls softens the contrast.

○ This combination works perfectly in simple checks and stripes, so look for fabrics such as old-fashioned mattress ticking and gingham in navy and white or black and white.

○ For more decoration and a less nautical feel, seek out classical monochrome patterns such as toile de Jouy that provide detailed figurative images with a traditionally elegant feel.

○ Soften the restrained, understated effect of the colors with fabric flourishes such as bed drapes and canopies or architectural details like archways and alcoves.

○ To add warmth without introducing color to the room, opt for a plain wood or terra-cotta floor.

INDEX

PHOTOGRAPHIC ACKNOWLEDGMENTS

Caroline Arber: pages 36 left, 52 top right, 108 left, 109 left, 109 right, 114 left, 122, 129, 153
Jan Baldwin: pages 38, 78 right
Tim Beddow: pages 31, 39
Mark Bolton: page 125
Charlie Colmer: pages 1, 21 right, 29, 35 left, 51 top right, 51 bottom right, 55, 64, 67, 70, 78 left, 79 top left, 81, 83 bottom, left, 88, 92, 95, 137 right, 138 left, 147 left, 155
Christopher Drake: pages 110 bottom, 143 left, 154
Andreas von Einsiedel: page 140 top right
Laurie Evans: page 113 top left
Craig Fordham: pages 47, 58
Kate Gadsby: page 123
Georgia Glynn Smith: pages 54 top right, 102-103
Catherine Gratwicke: pages 24 bottom left, 33, 54 bottom, 56, 61 right, 133, 140 left, 141 left, 145
Gridley and Graves: page 100
Scott Hawkins: page 26
Huntley Hedworth: pages 23 left, 32, 52 bottom, 65, 71, 138 right, 139 right, 141 right, 143 right, 150, 151 right
Ray Kachatorian: page 11
Sandra Lane: pages 42, 68
Tom Leighton: pages 59, 84, 97, 126, 142, 156
Michael Luppino: pages 2, 83 right, 148

Mark Luscombe White: pages 24 bottom right, 66
Charles Maraia: page 100
James Merrell: pages 17, 20 top left, 20 right, 23 left, 23 right, 24 top left, 24 top right, 25, 28 left, 30, 34, 36 right, 37, 41, 44-45, 53 bottom, 54 top left, 57 right, 62, 63, 75, 80 top left, 80 top right, 86, 89, 91, 93, 111 bottom left, 112 top left, 112 bottom, 118, 121 bottom, 124, 127, 136 right, 144, 147 right, 149, 151 left
Tham Nhu Tran: pages 43, 52 top left, 53 top left, 69, 72-73, 79 right, 85 left, 98, 115
Bridget Peirson: pages 60, 61 left, 111 top left, 121 top
Nick Pope: page 117
Alex Ramsay: page 136 left
Steven Randazzo: pages 5, 7
Kim Sayer: pages 14-15
Bob Smith: pages 8-9, 20 bottom left, 90, 128
Ron Sutherland: page 23 right
Debi Treloar: pages 35 right, 40, 57 left, 80 bottom, 108 right, 111 top right, 113 right, 114 right, 146
Pia Tryde: pages 13, 28 right, 50 left, 82 left, 87, 96, 99, 110 top, 111 bottom right, 116, 120
Simon Upton: pages 119, 139 left, 157
Peter Williams: page 105
Peter Woloszynski: page 22 left
Polly Wreford: pages 51 top left, 94, 152